INTERNATIONAL RECRUITMENT, SELECTION AND ASSESSMENT

Professor Paul Sparrow

The Chartered Institute of Personnel and Development is the leading publisher of books and reports for personnel and training professionals, students, and all those concerned with the effective management and development of people at work.
For full details of all our titles, please contact the Publishing Department:

Tel: 020 8612 6204

E-mail: publish@cipd.co.uk

To view and purchase all CIPD titles:
www.cipd.co.uk/bookstore

For details of CIPD research projects:
www.cipd.co.uk/research

INTERNATIONAL RECRUITMENT, SELECTION AND ASSESSMENT

Professor Paul Sparrow
LANCASTER UNIVERSITY MANAGEMENT SCHOOL

First published 2006

Cover and text design by Sutchinda Rangsi-Thompson
Typeset by Paperweight
Printed in Great Britain by Antony Rowe

British Library Cataloguing in Publication Data
A catalogue record for this book is available from the British Library

ISBN   1 84398 169 6
ISBN-13   978 1 84398 169 5

Chartered Institute of Personnel and Development,
151 The Broadway, London SW19 1JQ

Tel: 020 8612 6200
Website: www.cipd.co.uk

Incorporated by Royal Charter. Registered charity no. 1079797.

CONTENTS

ACKNOWLEDGEMENTS

The CIPD would like to thank Professor Paul Sparrow, author of this report.

Thanks also go to Vice President, International, Martin Ferber and previous Vice Presidents, Bob McCall and Bob Morton for their support of this project.

The CIPD is very appreciative of those companies and individuals who, taking the time to be interviewed for the case studies, have made this research possible.

Frances Wilson
Manager, International

FOREWORD

This research report is important because it focuses on changes in sourcing issues which many firms, not just those working internationally, are now facing. As a consequence, their HR professionals are confronting very different international recruitment, selection and assessment issues as they pick up the challenge of the rapidly expanding global labour market. No more do we just think about expatriation in the context of an international management development tool or a means of filling a short-term talent need overseas. Paul Sparrow's fascinating research looks at the increase in mobility of all different types of international employees, not just traditional overseas assignees.

The report looks at sourcing for roles overseas and also bringing talent from overseas to work in the home market. The rapid expansion of blurred labour markets means that HR people need to adapt rapidly to cope with increasingly complex demands. Skills shortages mean that certain sectors (for example, the NHS, hotel and catering, and retail) are looking outside the UK to fill posts. Statistics indicate that over 300,000 new workers have entered the UK labour market from new EU accession countries since 2004. Other international companies are looking to scale up very rapidly overseas, to shift resources and develop talent in unknown markets. Some of the challenges relating to this include understanding the vocational education and training qualification structures of these countries, assessing skills and competencies, and integrating diverse cultures into the workforce for individual and organisational effectiveness.

The government has embarked on a process of 'managed migration', with a range of legislative changes that HR professionals will have to understand and implement in their organisations. The construction industry, for example, reckons that at least 5% of the 88,000 new entrants needed over the next five years will be non-UK nationals. This involves many issues, including health and safety and comparability of qualifications, that need to be tackled.

Whichever aspect of managing global resourcing you are responsible for, this research report has the latest academic thinking and relevant case-study examples to provide great insight into this fascinating and challenging aspect of people management.

Martin Ferber
Vice President, International

EXECUTIVE SUMMARY

The HR function in international organisations has to meet a series of challenges. This Research Report draws three key conclusions about the role of HR professionals working in the field of international recruitment, selection and assessment:

1   The added value of the HR function in an international firm lies in its ability to manage the delicate balance between globally co-ordinated systems and sensitivity to local needs, including cultural differences, in a way that aligns both with business needs and senior management philosophy.

2   There is a distinction to be made now between international HRM and global HRM.

3   The old functional divides between international recruitment, international management development and international reward management have become increasingly weak. The solution to all the above challenges requires multiple actions covering all of these functions.

International recruitment, selection and assessment is carried out now in very different contexts, and it is these contexts that are used to structure the report.

FOUR KEY CONTEXTS FOR INTERNATIONAL RECRUITMENT, SELECTION AND ASSESSMENT

This report examines the following four contexts through the use of detailed case studies.

1   International recruitment from overseas countries for employment in the home (UK) market: *The case study looks at the experiences of South East*

London Strategic Health Authority, because it, along with the National Health Service in general, has operated a number of programmes to attract overseas candidates into the UK. The case study shows how the activity of the HR function shifts as it works its way through the initial challenges of attracting and recruiting overseas professionals, on to the longer-term issues associated with managing this cadre of overseas recruits through the organisation's career systems.

2   Resourcing specialist skills for use in home and overseas markets: *The case study looks at the experiences of the BBC World Service (part of the BBC's Global News division), which has to resource very specialist technical skills for deployment in overseas markets and at the same time manage a strong employer brand. The case looks at the recruitment, selection and assessment activity inside the HR function and then moves on to examine the changes taking place, because a range of HR activities, including some aspects of international recruitment, are now being outsourced as the BBC shifts towards a shared-service model.*

3   Recruitment in the context of an internationalisation strategy: *The case study looks at the experiences of Barclaycard International as it sets up operations in a series of new countries, part of its strategy to expand massively the scale of international business activity. The case study focuses on the necessary activity needed to ensure more expatriate mobility, a smooth process of new-country start-ups and changes in the role of in-country HR partners.*

4 Devolving responsibility for international recruitment: *The case study looks at the experiences of Save the Children UK and learning from the not-for-profit sector. The challenge here is how to combine diversity priorities with central needs for talent management. The case study examines the way in which Save the Children has decentralised responsibility for its international recruitment activity.*

The four case studies that form the core of this research are detailed and have been structured to demonstrate the main issues for International HR professionals when operating in each context. Data were gathered from February 2005 to March 2006.

In addition to this primary research into these four contexts, the report also pulls together other recent research, academic literature and accounts of practice. An evidence-based approach has been taken. There is a wealth of material in the forms of professional opinion, employer surveys and analyses of options that have been produced by professional bodies and service providers. It is always difficult to pick out any one study, and where this has been done it is purely to provide some grounding data around the issue under discussion. Such work is used to examine, for example, expatriate trends, employer branding strategies and levels of employee engagement.

At various points in the report, evidence from the academic literature and empirical studies is also used to aid understanding. In particular, there are sections on:

- expatriates as a source of international resourcing

- the skills associated with international management

- the assumptions that underlie our models

- the nature of global leadership

- the role of international management teams and requisite skills in cross-cultural communication

- self-initiated movers

- evidence of skills shortages, sources of international migration and regulatory changes

- local sensitivity issues, such as points of difference across countries in recruitment systems and issues to do with the use of tests across cultures

- usage of various tools and techniques.

Consulting these background sources will provide sufficient additional information, but on occasion under the label 'Where can I find out more?' specific guidance to sources of information is provided.

INTRODUCTION

❖ **The debate has moved on a long way since the 1999 report**

❖ **HR business partners have to balance consistency of policies with local sensitivities**

❖ **The phrase 'international employee' has changed its meaning**

❖ **International recruitment is no longer just about managing groups of expatriates**

❖ **The range of expertise-providers in this field has grown enormously – so who to talk to for advice?**

This report outlines some of the key findings from research and analysis on the challenges facing organisations in dealing with international recruitment, selection and assessment. Seven years ago a similar piece of work was carried out, looking at the policies and practices of a number of organisations and the offerings of a number of service providers in the field.[1]

❖ What has changed since then?

❖ Which debates remain the same?

❖ What are organisations doing about it?

At a surface level, many of the technical debates have remained the same regarding the tools and techniques that are brought to bear around candidate engagement, headhunting, graduate programmes, advertising, screening, testing, assessment and socialisation. However, as this report outlines, there has been substantial internationalisation both in the use of these tools and techniques and also in the structure and role of the HR departments that use them. This report has to cover a lot of material, as a recent review on designing and implementing global staffing systems noted:

> ...There is a great deal of resistance to designing and implementing global systems and policies because 'people are different', 'laws are different' and 'labour markets are different'. As the complexity of designing and implementing effective HR systems on an international scale cannot be denied, there are many areas where HR professionals have shied away from going global, preferring instead to implement local or regional solutions. However ... as more organisations begin to operate on a global (or at least multinational) scale, the need for HR systems that can be used across multiple countries continues to grow.[2]

Since 1999 a number of new tools and techniques have become part of the mainstream armoury of HR functions. In particular, there has been a very strong marketing, corporate communications and IT influence on the HR function. Indeed, one of the main findings from a recent research study on the impact of globalisation on HR functions is that it leads to new relationships between these corporate functions and the development of many hybrid professionals capable of using the tools and techniques of each function.[3] This convergence of thinking has brought the language of employee value propositions, employer branding, corporate social responsibility, market-mapping and recruiting ahead of the curve into the mix of HR activity. The challenge now is to try to manage these approaches on a global scale.

A common theme throughout the report is the challenge on the one hand of providing some degree of consistency (through either standardisation or optimisation) of practices around the world so that the organisation is using the same tools and techniques to obtain candidates who increasingly act as part of a more global community, and on the other hand of maintaining locally responsive and differentiated approaches. In some instances the pressures to differentiate staffing practices across countries or regions is unwarranted and can be 'defused' by ensuring that the legitimacy of the reasons to differentiate is determined and debated sensibly (these days with more of an onus on countries and regions to prove that they are different rather than with corporate functions to prove that they are right), that new or standardised approaches are market-tested, that there is insight into the legal issues in different countries, and that there are effective change management skills present across country operations. In order to ensure that the correct balance of standardisation versus differentiation is reached, geographical partners have to be treated as equal partners in the debate. Often it is the local in-country HR business partner who has to manage these tensions. Consequently, attention will also be given to their role in the process in this report.

It is important to signal, too, that although this report focuses on International recruitment, selection and assessment, the phrase 'global community' signals that we think very differently these days about what is meant by 'international employee'. Our definitions have become ever more varied. Consider for a moment whether the following categories of employee need the same sort of international skills and competencies:

- international commuters

- contract expatriates

- employees used on long-term business trips

- assignees on short-term or intermediate-term foreign postings

- a permanent cadre of global managers

- international transferees (moving from one subsidiary to another)

- self-initiated movers who live in a third country but are willing to work for a multinational

- virtual international employees active in cross-border project teams

- domestically based employees in a service centre who deal with overseas customers, suppliers and partners on a regular basis

- immigrants attracted to a domestic labour market.

The reality today is that there are many paths that organisations can follow to resource global labour needs. Consequently, in terms of global workforce planning, organisations often prefer to talk today about international employees (IEs) rather then the more traditional idea of expatriates and the associated categorisation of international assignees into parent country nationals, host country nationals or third country nationals. The days of brokering expatriates around the world and having specialist HR functions just to handle this small cadre of managers are rapidly being supplemented by other forms of professional HR expertise.

> ... the tradition of referring to all international employees as expatriates – or even international assignees – falls short of the need for international HR professionals to understand the options available ... and fit them to evolving international business strategies.[4]

'...for many HR functions the challenge they face is to help their organisation expand into new international markets.'

Another challenge today is the speed at which the need to recruit internationally develops and the volatility of the activities that are involved. This can be demonstrated by a quick analysis of typical business headlines. Consider the following developments, evidenced by reports in one day's edition of the *Financial Times*.[5] They show that for many HR functions the challenge they face is to help their organisation expand into new international markets. New operations are being established and then possibly scaled down again, restructured or even disposed of. For example:

1 Many of the global retail chains have long wanted to enter developing markets. Tesco has been lobbying to enter the Indian market for several years – it already sources £65 million of goods a year from India. The size of the middle class has been growing by 20 million a year – a huge business opportunity. Carrefour moved into the South Korean market in 1996 but its business has been underperforming. It withdrew from the Japanese market to concentrate on China and now might withdraw from the third largest Asian market of Korea. Wal-Mart and Samsung Tesco are waiting in the wings to acquire its stores but will face competition from Shinsegae, the largest domestic retailer.[6] Similarly, the retail banks have an aspiration to move into developing countries and have declared publicly their intention to move into markets such as India, Russia and China.

2 A number of organisations running service operations have to re-organise their call centre operations, moving employment around the globe. As part of its strategy to improve operating margins to 10% and in response to greater e-enablement of purchasing, British Airways has begun to close more of its UK call centres. UK call centre employment has fallen from 2,200 to 800, out of a global workforce of 2,100. Two UK centres will remain as part of a worldwide network of 14, with operations in Germany, the US and India. One of the main reasons, however, is that online bookings have doubled in two years to form 30% of all bookings, and they are expected to reach 50% in two years' time. Phone calls to UK call centres have fallen from 15 to 6 million in the same time.

3 Lloyds TSB closed three UK processing and administration sites as work gravitates towards fewer but larger centres. A further 105 jobs are being transferred to India, and employment in India will grow from 2,000 to 2,750 by the end of 2006.

Traditionally, international HRM has been about managing an international workforce – the expatriates, frequent commuters, cross-cultural team members and specialists involved in international knowledge transfer. Global HRM is not simply about covering these staff around the world. It is about managing international HRM activities through the application of global rule-sets. Attention needs to be devoted to understanding the ways in which the HR function itself contributes to the process of globalisation, because:

> globalisation occurs at the level of the function, rather than the firm.[7]

Not only has international recruitment and resourcing moved away from its traditional focus on managing pools of expatriates, given the changing structure and role of International HR functions, but HR functions and their HR Business Partners now also have to help their organisations manage a very wide range of issues.

KEY DEVELOPMENTS THAT BRING INTERNATIONAL RESOURCING CHALLENGES

❖ consequences of global business process redesign, the pursuit of a global centre of excellence strategy and the global re-distribution and re-location of work that this often entails

❖ absorption of acquired businesses, merging of existing operations on a global scale, the staffing of strategic integration teams, and attempts to develop and harmonise core HR processes within these merged businesses

❖ rapid start-up of international operations and organisation development as they mature through different stages of the business life-cycle

❖ changing capabilities of international operations with increased needs for up-skilling of local operations and greater complexity of their business models

❖ need to capitalise on the potential that technology affords the delivery of HR through shared services, on a global basis, while ensuring that local social and cultural insights are duly considered when it is imperative to do so

❖ changes being wrought in the HR service supply chain as the need for several intermediary service providers is being reduced, and as web-based HR provision increases

❖ articulation of appropriate pledges about the levels of performance that can be delivered to the business by the IHR function, and the requirement to meet these pledges under conditions of cost control

❖ learning about operating through formal or informal global HR networks, acting as knowledge brokers across international operations, and avoiding a 'one best way' HR philosophy

❖ offering a compelling value proposition to the employees of the firm, and understanding and then marketing the brand that the firm represents across global labour markets that in practice have different values and different perceptions

❖ identity problems faced by HR professionals as they experience changes in the level of decentralisation/centralisation across constituent international businesses, as knowledge and ideas about best practice flows from the centre to the operations and vice versa

The recruitment and selection function has experienced particularly rapid global exposure. In response to the above trends, and in addition to the traditional requirement to manage a cadre of internationally mobile managers, a number of new streams of activity may now have to managed from within the HR function:

> 'There is a very significant challenge facing organisations now having to understand the vocational education and training qualification structures of other countries...'

1 The enlargement of the European Union (EU) has opened up many new product and service markets, but also of course new labour markets in Eastern Europe. In response to skills shortages in their domestic markets, many organisations have begun to attract more international labour to their home markets or to new overseas operations, often from new and little understood labour markets. Some 300,000 new workers from new EU accession countries have entered the UK labour market. There is a very significant challenge facing organisations now having to understand the vocational

education and training qualification structures of other countries, and especially the hidden strengths and weaknesses that these systems create in terms of employee skills and capabilities.

2 There is a shift in responsibilities taking place in terms of international resourcing. The forthcoming shift to a skills-based points system for immigration means that the government now sees migration as necessary in supporting sustainable economic growth and addressing skills shortages. It has embarked on a process of 'managed migration' which, in addition to a package of legislative changes, also involves building public understanding of this need and consultation with employers and trade unions about migration policies. This international migration – and the associated need to conduct short term recruitment trawls in overseas countries – has led to the development of new activities and new professional skills in many HR functions.

3 We have seen the transfer of work abroad with the growth of outsourcing, offshoring or global in-sourcing. It is easy to overstate the scale of this (for example, analyses suggest that for the USA perhaps 3% of their jobs might move offshore), but for many HR functions it does create the requirement to recruit and manage a workforce overseas.

4   Yet at the same time, the competition for staff who *are* perceived to be talented has become more intense. Organisations have extended their talent pipelines to ever earlier stages of the skills formation process, attempting to influence the syllabuses and conduct of national vocational education and training systems across the geographies that they represent. This linkage of international recruitment activity with more strategic concerns is leading to a broadened set of activities that have to be managed by HR functions and HR business partners.

> 'A key requirement for HR professionals is to identify where to look, who to trust and work with, and how to use the information...'

To add one last issue to what can be seen to be an ever more complex role, the source of knowledge and expertise about these sorts of activities has become very fragmented. Who do you talk to to find out how best to handle these challenges? The knowledge has long since moved out of many HR functions. Key service providers such as headhunters, advertising agencies and consulting firms have always played a key role in international recruitment, selection and assessment activities. However, today, as a consequence both of outsourcing of activity from HR functions and the creation of the new streams of activity outlined above, there is now a plethora of services and expertise-providers operating in the market. Advice can be sought on: how to research and map out markets and identify talented executives, through to how to manage your web profile if you are an executive; how to source employees from developing markets, through to how to work in the UK and then broker your skills and build your career back in a developing country; how to build a corporate and pan-geographical employer brand, through to how to identify the local sensitivities that will dilute the power of any such brand. A key requirement for HR professionals is to identify where to look, who to trust and work with, and how to use the information that may be provided. This report attempts to help collate and signpost some of this expertise.

A final issue concerns the alternative ways in which organisations might resource their international business activity without having actually to recruit anyone. Although this report focuses on the challenges of international recruitment, perhaps not surprisingly, organisations are doing their best to avoid the need to bring in more international recruits, generally by relying on other solutions such as using international management teams and providing co-ordination through international managers who travel frequently. Some brief mention is therefore made in the report about these developments as well. So, what is known about the different types of international employee and the skills and competencies that they need?

ENDNOTES

1   IPD (1999). *The IPD Guide on International Recruitment, Selection and Assessment*. London: CIPD.

2   Ryan, A.M., Wiechmann, D. and Hemingway, M. (2003) Designing and implementing global staffing systems: Part II. Best practices. *Human Resource Management*. Vol. 42, No. 1. 85–94, p. 85.

3   Sparrow, P.R., Brewster, C. and Harris, H. (2004) *Globalizing Human Resource Management*. London: Routledge.

4   Briscoe, D. and Schuler, R.S. (2004). *International Human Resource Management*. 2nd edn. New York: Routledge. p. 223.

5   See: Done, K. (2006) BA takes flight from the High Street. *Financial Times*. 16 March. p. 19; Croft, J. (2006) Lloyds TSB closes processing centres. *Financial Times*. 16 March. p. 23; Fifield, A. (2006) Rivals eye Carrefour Korea stores. *Financial Times*. 16 March. p. 25.

6   *Daily Telegraph* (2005) Tesco bids to enter Indian market. *Daily Telegraph Business News*. 15 November.

7   Malbright, T. (1995) Globalisation of an ethnographic firm, *Strategic Management Journal*. Vol. 16. 119–41, p. 119.

TYPES OF INTERNATIONAL EMPLOYEE AND THEIR REQUIRED COMPETENCIES   1

❖ **Competing theories about the selection criteria for expatriates**

❖ **Assumptions about the skills that international managers need**

❖ **Global managers as opposed to expatriate managers**

❖ **What is an 'international mindset'?**

❖ **Some alternatives to long-term expatriation**

In this chapter the main evidence for the skills and competencies that become important when people operate internationally is examined along with the latest thinking on the issue. A key point needs to be made immediately, especially given the comments in the Introduction. Looking at the different assumptions that we make about the skills and competencies that are needed by international employees, one could be forgiven for saying: 'But this is only important for large organisations that employ a small cadre of internationally mobile managers and expatriates. We are simply sourcing employees in different parts of the world and would never recruit for these sorts of competency.' However, if we look at what we know about the use of international employees in general, it becomes clear that organisations do indeed still need to think about such skills, and at surprisingly low levels of their organisation.

The CIPD *Guide on International Management Development* (2005) covers many of the issues associated with expatriation, so attention here is focused more directly on the implications for international recruitment. A series of questions is generally asked about the recruitment of international employees:[1]

❖ Can the competencies that become important for international management be developed?

❖ Are some competencies so complex, rare on the ground or time-consuming to build that the real issue is to select and motivate a small elite of managers?

❖ Can we identify a clear hierarchy of international management skills, from the most basic, to higher levels of performance and sophistication, or must we be left with endless lists of desirable characteristics with assumed relevance?

❖ Do internal resourcing systems realistically make such graded and calibrated decisions about managers?

❖ Are line managers just happy to find candidates who are half-competent, but are willing and mobile?

> '…it *is* possible to specify a set of competencies for the international manager…'

The consensus view from HR practitoners for some time now is that it *is* possible to specify a set of competencies for the international manager, and that these can be used to assist the selection of some people in some jobs. However, there are different views about the practicality of using these to select international managers and most certainly the feasibility of developing the full spectrum of international management competencies in a sufficiently large pool of employees. Seven years ago the first guide in this area reported two competing resourcing philosophies:

1   the traditional psychometric approach, whereby role analyses and corporate competency systems recognise the importance of competencies associated with international management; these are then used to predict individuals' suitability for assignment

2   a clinical risk-assessment approach, which investigates the individual psychological transitions and adaptations that international managers have to undergo, but which, recognising that there is no choice but for that person to undertake the assignment, directs attention to the design of the assignment around the manager in order to minimise risks to the organisation.

The first, traditional 'psychometric', approach argued that there is an identifiable set of competencies that are associated with success and that these can be used to predict effective performers in international roles. Few professionals doubted that selecting someone for an international assignment drew attention to quite stringent criteria, and that there was a tension between the skills and competencies that organisations thought they should be looking at when they recruited, and the skills that were actually needed to make a success of working abroad. It was also accepted that factors that became essential when operating internationally, such as openness to experience, tolerance of ambiguity, introversion, the ability to generate and inspire trust in others, and proactive information-seeking, could be understated in domestic selection systems, and that they therefore had to be given some attention when internationalising the organisation.

The second philosophy, the 'clinical risk-assessment approach', found favour among professionals who argued that there were limits to using personal competencies as a selection criterion for international employees. The reasons for the failure of international management assignments often go beyond problems of the managers' cultural adaptability, maturity and stability. Adaptability of the partner, dual-career difficulties, national attitudes to mobility and pay arrangements clearly all play a role in the success of the assignment.

Similarly, the supporting structures that surrounded the international manager (in terms of localisation policies, management structures, reporting relationships, accountabilities and responsibilities, and the technical difficulty of assignment) all played a part. Developments associated with the business needed

far greater cost-control over international managers, and changes in the position power of international managers (related to the growth of joint ventures and strategic alliances) all meant that the supply (or lack of supply) of willing employees limited the selection context. Finally, while professionals accepted that international assignments required significant psychological adaptation, the use of competencies was thought to be too cumbersome in an international recruitment and selection setting, might not actually be predictive of success, or was simply too difficult to measure reliably based on the quality of data made available to HR managers in a field setting.

This dilemma and difference in view still exists, but on the basis of more recent work on international resourcing and on feedback gained in this research, it is clear that opinion continues to shift towards the practicality of the second philosophy.

EXPATRIATES AS A SOURCE OF INTERNATIONAL RESOURCING AND MOBILITY

In part, this shift has occurred because organisations use expatriates as part of an international resourcing strategy in very different ways (see box below).

THE DIFFERENT WAYS IN WHICH EXPATRIATES ARE USED AS PART OF A RESOURCING STRATEGY

An analysis of company practice with regard to the role of expatriates to assist international resourcing signposts five different types of organisation:[2]

❖ *Global*: The archetypal role in large global multinationals with established reputations for expatriate management. Comprehensive sets of procedures in place, centres of excellence to manage knowledge about best practice. Expatriation expected by employees to form the basis of a professional and managerial career inside the organisation. Being an expat seen as a necessary part of career path to senior roles in the organisation. Recruitment and selection systems concentrate on internal labour market.

❖ *Emissary*: Organisations have established overseas markets and a long-term view as to their positioning. However, resourcing systems are firmly rooted in the domestic home culture. Expatriates may be excused from international assignments, but have a role to represent the power and ideology of the headquarters and export its systems. Assignments act as a mission away from the corporate centre. Comprehensive back-up provided to compensate for the burden of an overseas post. Key challenge is to maintain motivation of candidates.

❖ *Peripheral:* Characteristic of companies operating in geographies where expatriation is a sought-after option and a reward in its own right. Globalisation process resulting in new international expansion opportunities. Limited growth opportunities in home market, and overseas assignments seen as a perk, facilitating the temporary migration of candidates to overseas posts. Domestic workforce might itself be sourced from several countries and be multi-ethnic, and so ample employees willing to be dispersed throughout the world.

❖ *Professional*: A preference to use external people and buy-in expertise and knowledge, in effect outsourcing the expatriation process. Goal is to concentrate on home-country strengths and keep people within specified geographical borders. Skills bought in from external labour market at the periphery of the organisation. Expatriates hired to act as 'foreign legion troopers' and have careers that span expatriate assignments in several companies. Recruitment and selection focused around work history and previous assignments rather than personal skills and attributes. Cost-driven and transactional psychological contract. Critical issues concern loyalty and commitment.

❖ *Expedient*: An emergent approach for organisations newly internationalising and developing policies and procedures. Ad hoc and pragmatic choices across the other policies.

SKILLS ASSOCIATED WITH EXPATRIATE OR INTERNATIONAL MANAGERS

The evidence on international management skills has been examined by a number of writers. In terms of the skills, competencies and behaviours that are needed, a distinction is typically made between the:

❖ expatriate (or international) manager: an executive in a leadership position that involves international assignments in different countries and cultures, with skills defined by the location of the assignment

❖ global (or transnational) manager: an executive assigned to positions with cross-border responsibilities, who has a hands-on understanding of international business, with skills defined more by their frame of mind.

Some global managers may be expatriates; many, if not most, have been expatriates at some point in their career, but probably only a few expatriates are global managers.[3]

Research on the first group, expatriates, still tends to regard their role as part of an international resourcing strategy from the perspective of multinationals. The consensus is that:

Although expatriates are costly, staff transfers remain a valuable strategic tool: as an informal control mechanism, for knowledge transfer, and for international team development.[4]

There are, however, immense difficulties in ensuring that there is a sufficient pool of motivated expatriates. Ultimately, selection systems for international employees have to make a trade-off between competency versus commitment. Ideally, both needs can be satisfied, but a competent yet unwilling expatriate is as damaging to business as a committed but incompetent one!

> '...a competent yet unwilling expatriate is as damaging to business as a committed but incompetent one.'

Most studies have dealt with the skills needed for expatriate managers – focusing on lists of criteria, competencies and personal characteristics that should be assessed as part of the selection criteria. Studies have also analysed the reasons for assignment failure and recommended the HR practices that can help organisations select, develop and retain competent expatriate managers. A recent review of the expatriate literature and analysis of the skills necessary for cross-cultural learning identified 73 skills that clustered into 10 high-level competencies.[5]

A key observation for those concerned with the early identification of international management potential from this work is that many of the lessons learned about the recruitment of expatriates can be generalised to people working in other international contexts. The majority of expatriate skills are learned through experience – they learn how to manage across cultures in most instances without training or education in cross-cultural

skills. So too must international managers who, while not having to become totally immersed in a new culture because they are an expatriate, encounter individuals of different cultures through overseas trips to customers or suppliers, short visits to international operations, or work in international management teams. Increasingly, these managers too can no longer work in the comfort of their home culture.[6]

The broad situation in terms of characteristics to be considered include the following:[7]

CHARACTERISTICS OF THE SUCCESSFUL EXPATRIATE MANAGER

Professional and technical competence and experience on the job:
Experience in the company
Technical knowledge of the business
Previous overseas experience
Managerial talent
Overall experience and education

Relational ability 1: Personality traits and relational abilities:
Communicative ability and interpersonal skills
Maturity and emotional stability
Tolerance for ambiguity in personal relations, unfamiliar situations/new experiences
Behavioural and attitudinal flexibility: willingness to acquire new patterns
Respect for culture of host country
Adaptability and flexibility in new environment

Relational ability 2: Perceptual dimensions and life strategies:
Information-seeking skills: listening and observation
Modelling capacities: draws upon observational learning to acquire knowledge, attitudes, values, emotional proclivities and competences
Non-judgemental frameworks
Non-evaluative in interpreting the behaviour of host-country nationals

Self-maintenance factors:
Ability to substitute traditional reinforcements with other activities
Stress-reduction techniques
Self-maintenance, confidence in one's ability to perform specific behaviours (self-efficacy)

Leadership and motivational factors:
Relationship development and personal influence skills
Willingness to communicate
Action and initiative skills
Belief in the mission
Interest in overseas experience
Congruence with career path

Cultural awareness:

Cultural robustness: has an understanding of the differences between countries

Host-country language skills and translation of concepts, ideas and thoughts in verbal form

Understanding non-verbal communication

Family situation:

Stability of family situation

Spouse and family's adaptability and supportiveness

The important questions, however, are: can these competencies be acquired through learning and training; are all the competencies essential; and is everyone equally trainable?

Organisations that face short lead times prior to commencement of international assignments (and hence cannot provide pre-departure cross-cultural training) can benefit greatly from a framework that helps determine which competencies will most effectively help expatriates to 'hit the ground running' and which competencies may be acquired later, through on-the-job learning.[15]

Broadly speaking, the competencies in Figure 1, opposite, reflect the KSAO (Knowledge, Skills, Ability and Other) categorisation familiar in the domestic HRM literature. The knowledge and skills represent dynamic competencies that may be acquired through training on or off the job, and ability and personality factors represent more stable competencies because they are relatively fixed and constrain the potential to learn a new skill. The stable skills are therefore considered to be essential for international managers if they are to learn subsequently from experience.

A recent review of the field argued that if we are to move beyond our currently limited views of the skills needed by people operating in this environment, then we need more research that employs longitudinal designs and that also includes the host-country perspective on the determinants, processes and outcomes of international adjustment.[8] From a theoretical perspective, our models of international management skills can be classified as being driven by four sets of assumptions as described in the box below, about learning, stress-coping, development and personality.

A recent study has collated evidence across 66 studies that have looked at the role of 50 determinants and consequences of

THE ASSUMPTIONS ABOUT THE SKILLS NEEDED BY INTERNATIONAL MANAGERS

Learning models: These assume that the adjustments that international employees have to make (and therefore the skills and competencies that they need) have to do with learning new skills and techniques of adaptation; the impact of the 'other' culture can be seen as a change in behavioural reinforcement contingencies. The major task facing expatriates is to adjust their social skills in such a way that they can learn the salient characteristics of the new environment in terms of new roles, rules and norms of social interaction. Cross-cultural training is generally designed on the principle that the rules and values of a new culture have to be learned (and a repertoire of cognitive and behavioural schema and responses developed) before adjustment can take place.[9]

Stress-coping models: These assume that feelings of anxiety, confusion and disruption associated with culture shock are akin to individual stress reactions under conditions of uncertainty, information overload and loss of control. The adjustment reaction is characterised by a variety of symptoms of psychological distress associated with any critical life event. Moreover, role theory argues that competing assignment demands make role conflicts unavoidable, and it is this that affects effectiveness. Stress management (coping strategies), rather than stress avoidance, is necessary in order for expatriates to engage in necessary engagement behaviours.[10] International employees have to draw on a wide range of such strategies to manage problems, although there may not be congruence between what is necessary to manage stress and what is required for effective management of the assignment.

Developmental models: These assume that there is a series of phases of adjustment that an international employee has to go through (for example, contact, disintegration, reintegration, autonomy and independence) that reflect progressive stages of cultural awareness.[11] Individuals undertake adaptive activities only when environmental challenges threaten their internal equilibrium. Processes of periodic (rather than linear) disintegration, regrouping/regeneration, and then higher maturation (progressive inter-cultural sensitivity often also associated with global leadership competence) are an inevitable consequence of exposure to other cultures. In a rare qualitative study of returned expatriate stories,[12] researchers adapted the metaphor of heroic adventures to note the importance of personal transformations that accompany adjustment processes.

Personality-based models: These assume that such development can in part be predicted by a set of generalisable attitudes and traits, such as adaptation, cross-cultural and partnership skills[13] or personality variables that are associated with model cross-cultural collaborators. The importance of these prerequisites depends on the nature of the position and task variables, organisation characteristics and host country. Empirical support is, however, still weak, and again there may be contradictions between what is required for interaction adjustment and work adjustment. Moreover, as found in a study of German international employees assigned to work in Japan and the USA, each country presented different problems and conflicts to the employees and therefore required differential personality-related coping strategies.[14]

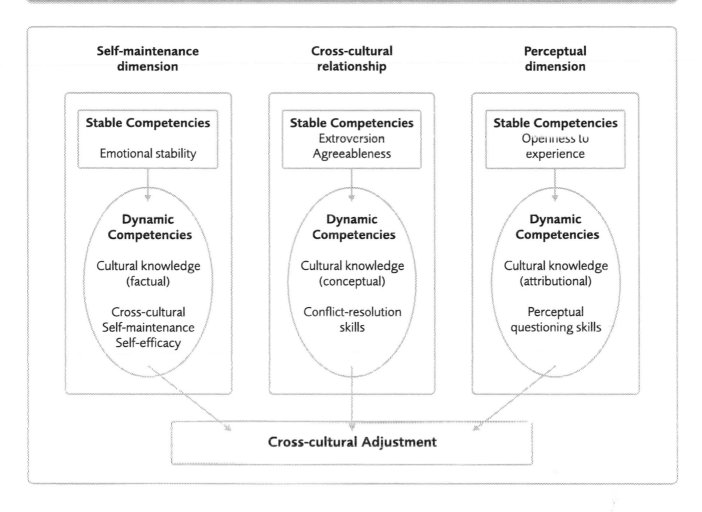

Figure 1 ❖ **The dynamic and stable cross-cultural competencies model**

Self-maintenance dimension

Stable Competencies

Emotional stability

Dynamic Competencies

Cultural knowledge (factual)

Cross-cultural Self-maintenance Self-efficacy

Cross-cultural relationship

Stable Competencies
Extroversion
Agreeableness

Dynamic Competencies

Cultural knowledge (conceptual)

Conflict-resolution skills

Perceptual dimension

Stable Competencies
Openness to experience

Dynamic Competencies

Cultural knowledge (attributional)

Perceptual questioning skills

Cross-cultural Adjustment

adjustment in 8,474 expatriates. The study looked at the trajectory of adjustment over time and how this affected any adjustment. The results showed the centrality, criticality and complexity of adjustment and strongly supported the effect that it has on job satisfaction, withdrawal cognitions and performance.[16]

> 'Previous experience of international assignments had a minimal impact on subsequent adjustment.'

Language skills helped international managers engage in rewarding interpersonal exchanges but had no effect on work adjustment. Previous experience of international assignments had a minimal impact on subsequent adjustment. Two individual factors were important in predicting adjustment: the ability to be a self-starter, and relational skills, the latter exceeding other predictors by 30% in terms of explaining variance in adjustment. Finally, non-work factors such as culture novelty and spouse adjustment were extremely potent predictors of successful overseas adjustment.

THE CHANGING CONTEXT FOR EXPATRIATE MANAGEMENT

A number of contextual factors are, then, clearly also important:

❖ From a host-country perspective, the significance of an international manager's role varies depending on the social and economic benefits that will come from the role; status implications; and what is expected of the role versus what the expatriate perceives to be important. The implication is that the interpretation of the level of international skills is heightened depending on how favourable (or not) these local perceptions are.

❖ In managing expatriates, partner mobility is also still a major problem. Where organisations cannot offer a favoured candidate the opportunity for their spouse to work, then the chances of recruitment are drastically reduced[17]. A number of developments are occurring aimed at freeing up restrictions on work permits for spouses. The European Commission has launched a discussion document on the management of economic migration. There are also professional bodies advancing company concerns, such as the not-for-profit Permits Foundation, which is encouraging governments to relax work permit regulations for the spouses or partners of expatriates.

❖ In order to increase levels of commitment, international managers also have to perceive that there is career value in expatriation. This perception can be an important predictor of their ability to make the above adjustments successfully. At the individual level, the top two motives for seeking and accepting an international assignment are the promise of financial incentives and career advancement. Examination of the experience of repatriation suggests that the ability of organisations to deliver on these promises is not always guaranteed.

> '**Rising costs, staff expectations and greater risks associated with certain locations mean that each assignment is increasingly viewed on the basis of a cost–benefit analysis.**'

The situation with regard to the use of expatriates as both a vanguard for international recruitment and as a form of 'corporate glue' has been changing quite rapidly in recent years. Rising costs, staff expectations and greater risks associated with certain locations mean that each assignment is increasingly viewed on the basis of a cost–benefit analysis. Many organisations are in the process of reconsidering the role of their internationally mobile employees.

WHERE CAN I FIND OUT MORE?

In the past five years there has been a proliferation of organisations providing statistical data and research reports on all aspects of expatriate management, ranging from current levels of mobility through to detailed expatriate policies and practices. Here are some of the better-known:

Centre for Research into the Management of Expatriation:

http://www.som.cranfield.ac.uk/som/research/centres/creme/publications.asp

Employment Conditions Abroad International (reports):

http://www.eca-international.com/

GMAC Global Relocation Services/ National Foreign Trade Council/ SHRM (reports):

http://www.gmacglobalrelocation.com/home.asp

ORC Worldwide:

http://www.orcinc.com/compensation/index.html

PriceWaterhouseCoopers International Assignments Global Policy and Practice Key Trends

http://www.pwccn.com/home/eng/tax_ia_keytrends2005.html

KPMG Global Assignment Policies and Practices Survey

http://www.kpmg.com.au/Default.aspx?TabID=214&KPMGArticleItemID=1626

Mercer International Assignments Survey

http://www.imercer.com/globalcontent/employeemobility/intlassign.asp

The situation can be summarised using one such survey by means of example. The latest GMAC survey suggests the following situation with regard to global mobility[18]:

❖ Around 40% of organisations deploy 50 or fewer expatriates, 9% from 51–100 expatriates, 13% up to 1,000, and 13% claim to have over 1,000 expatriates.

❖ Twenty-three per cent of expatriates now are women (up from 10% in 1994), and 54% are aged between 20 and 39 (compared to 41% in 1994).

❖ Family concerns and spouse career issues continue to dominate reasons for failure to accept an assignment and also assignment failure.

❖ Only around 12% of employees in the surveyed organisations were considered to have international experience.

❖ In 1997 81% of organisations expected an increase in their expatriate population, but the early 2000s also saw a period of cost-cutting (currently this may be easing a little). In 2001 only 23% of organisations expected growth in the size of their expatriate workforce, but by 2005 this had recovered to 47%.

❖ Formal cross-cultural training is made available to 20% of employees.

❖ Seventy per cent of organisations require a clear statement of objectives, 52% some kind of cost–benefit analysis, but only 37% compare estimated costs with actual costs and just 14% measure the return on investment.

> '**Expatriate attrition rates are at least double those of other employees…**'

Assignment failure is still reported as the most frequent problem in destinations such as China, Japan, the USA, the UK, Saudi Arabia and Iraq. Causes of assignment failure in order of importance are spouse/partner dissatisfaction, other family concerns, inability to adapt, job not meeting expectations, poor job performance, poor candidate selection, quality of life, dissatisfaction with remuneration, and security and safety issues. Expatriate attrition rates are at least double those of other employees, 21 per cent of expatriates leaving the organisation during the assignment, 23 per cent leaving within one year of return and 20 per cent leaving between the second and third years.

It was noted above that there are at least five different ways in which organisations tend to use expatriates as part of an international resourcing strategy: global, emissary, peripheral, professional or expedient. Of these, the professional option is associated with more external and contractualised management of expatriates. Associated with this development, a number of terms have arisen to describe mechanisms to house some or all of an organisation's globally mobile workforce.

These incorporated entities usually form part of an organisation's group structure and are referred to as employee leasing companies, offshore payroll companies, manpower companies or global employment companies (GECs)[19]. Fees are charged to internal businesses for the seconded services of employees and are used to pay salaries and benefits in the offshore company. They were originally used as a device to assist corporate tax departments manage transfer pricing and to minimise exposure to permanent establishment scrutiny.

As they also tend to house the HR functions associated with a global workforce, organisations are reportedly using GECs to serve as reservoirs of talent. The pool of talent can be mobilised while on assignment or be 'on hold' on repatriation before their deployment (or re-deployment), enabling easier succession and career planning. In some instances, the use of GECs is being used as a hiring incentive to career expatriates to offer more favourable tax-effective conditions of employment.

GLOBAL LEADERSHIP AND INTERNATIONAL MINDSET

In contrast to expatriates, global managers (or leaders) need to demonstrate global thinking or an international mindset. This places high value on sharing information, knowledge and experience across national, functional and business boundaries and on balancing the competing country, business and functional priorities that emerge as organisations globalise. The topic of global leadership continues to receive attention, not least because:

> as companies rely more and more on global strategies, they require more and more global leaders. This tie between strategy and leadership is essentially a two-way street: the more companies pursue global strategies, the more global leaders they need; and the more global leaders companies have, the more they pursue global strategies.[20]

However, few studies have looked at global leaders in detail, and the evidence still tends to be more anecdotal. A range of industrial perspectives in response to the pioneering work of Bartlett and Ghoshal have been provided recently by the chief executives of HSBC, Schering-Plough, General Electric, Flextronics and Egon Zehnder[21]. From a more academic perspective, attention has focused on the role played by both the social networks and also the superior cognitive processes possessed by global managers or leaders. The earliest debates on international management strategy argued that strategic capability is ultimately dependent on the 'cognitive processes' of international managers and the ability of firms to create a 'matrix in the minds of managers', or a transnational mentality[22]. Therefore, rather than just focusing on a particular skills-set or range of competencies, there are two important additional aspects to this 'mentality':

❖ attitudes/values

❖ cognitive structures.

The first component has been described as representing an 'attitudinal attribute' of an international orientation. This attitude is assumed to correlate with both the extent and the quality of international experience. Researchers have attempted to develop measures that correspond to the core dimensions of managers' thinking about international strategy and international organisation. They have then shown how this mindset changes over time[23] by looking, for example, at the type of cognitive change towards a more global mindset in managers over a three-year period within a single multinational organisation, identifying a core value-set or logic that is associated with global operations.

Global managers also need to have a 'good' *mental model of how knowledge and information is shared* across the people with whom they need to interact, if they are to deliver an important global business process, product or service. In this regard, expatriates have been seen as an important mechanism for knowledge capture and transfer inside global firms. In line with this, recent work has looked at:

❖ the role of expatriates as brokers of knowledge internationally and how they diffuse practices across borders

❖ the spread of tacit knowledge within top management teams through 'advice networks'

❖ factors that mitigate against the international transfer of knowledge through expatriates

❖ the 'social capital' that accrues to international managers as a consequence of their boundary-spanning roles

❖ knowledge sharing through interpersonal cross-border relationships[24].

> 'Cross-cultural studies have generally indicated a strong connection between national culture and preferred leadership styles.'

Not surprisingly, then, in the last few years there has been more detailed examination of global leadership styles and the impact of national culture upon these. Cross-cultural studies have generally indicated a strong connection between national culture and preferred leadership styles. The GLOBE project has made a contribution to the debate about the inter-relationships between societal culture, organisational culture and organisational leadership. This was a multi-phase, multi-method project that involved 170 social scientists and management academics[25]. The goal was to develop an empirically-based theory to describe, understand and predict the impact of cultural variables on leadership and organisational processes, and the effectiveness of these processes. The project asked four questions about global leadership:

1　Are there leader behaviours, attributes and organisational practices that are accepted and effective across cultures?

2 Are there leader behaviours, attributes and organisational practices that are accepted and effective only in some cultures?

3 How do attributes of societal and organisational cultures affect the kind of leader behaviours and organisational practices that are accepted and effective?

4 Can the universal and culture-specific aspects of leader behaviours, attributes and organisational practices be explained in terms of an underlying theory?

Nine dimensions of national culture were revealed, translated into questionnaire items that measured both what should be (ie, shared modal values of collectives), and what is or what are (ie, the common behaviours, institutional practices and prescriptions). They were distributed to middle managers in 62 national cultures. Ten distinct national clusters emerged within the overall sample, and a total of 23 different leadership styles were deemed to be effective in one or more of the different societal cultures of the world (each leadership style was considered to represent a *culturally endorsed implicit leadership theory, or CELT*). There were six underlying dimensions or styles of global leadership. The researchers drew a number of conclusions:

❖ There are subtle, but meaningful, variations in scores around leadership dimensions.

❖ However, the charismatic dimension (such attributes as visionary, inspirational, self-sacrificial, integrity, decisiveness and performance orientation) appeared to be universally rated as the most important leadership style.

❖ The interpretation of charisma in different societal settings was considered to vary.

❖ There was high within-culture agreement with respect to leader attributes and behaviours, and two out of six leader behaviour dimensions were viewed universally as contributors to effective leadership.

In short, there were 21 specific behaviours that were universal, 8 impediment behaviours, and 35 behaviours that depended upon the cultural context. Overall, the research supported the argument that leadership is culturally contingent, although the key dimensions of effective leadership are consistent across societal clusters.

Equally as important, global leaders need to possess some very specific skills and competencies simply because the roles that they perform are complex:

[Global leaders] have to possess a complex amalgamation of technical, functional, cultural, social and political competencies to navigate successfully the intricacies of changing cross-border responsibilities.[26]

Researchers looking at global leadership skills also make a distinction between the following sorts of capital that people need in these roles:

❖ social capital (which leads to trust)

❖ political capital (which leads to legitimacy)

❖ human capital (which leads to competencies)

❖ cultural capital (which leads to social inclusion and acceptance).

While many recruitment and selection systems focus on human capital (the skills and competencies needed for the job), external context factors have much to do with the building of international managers' social and political capital. A recent study of managers working in international teams, and the skills that were needed for the team to mutually adjust, showed that an expatriate's adjustment within a team is not influenced solely by his or her own competencies. Instead, the power balance between team members is likely to have a major influence on the course of adjustment.[27] Depending on the distribution of the nationality of headquarters, leadership and the customer interface, the expatriate will have more or less power to demand changes from the other side, and to achieve them through teaching and control.

> '...an expatriate's adjustment within a team is not influenced solely by his or her own competencies.'

The most recent question that has been asked by researchers is, 'Can organisations develop cultural intelligence among their employees?' This is an important part of global leadership skills, and it is also important for the effective functioning of international management teams. There has been a recent and important exchange of views between cross-cultural researchers[28] about the concept of Cultural Intelligence (CQ). This is an attitude and skill that enables individuals to adapt effectively across cultures. In practical terms, it enables an individual to interpret unfamiliar and ambiguous gestures in ways as accurately as a national compatriot could. Understanding the nature of CQ has important applications to individuals, teams and organisational functioning:

A person with high cultural intelligence can somehow tease out from a person's or group's behaviour those features that would be true of all people and all groups, those peculiar to this person or this group, and those that are neither universal nor idiosyncratic. The vast realm that lies between those two poles is culture.

Research on intercultural competence has a long tradition, and it shows that a range of factors can predict effectiveness in this area, including previous experience, personality factors, cross-cultural attitudes and communication behaviours, and situational factors such as cultural training or the 'distance' between two cultures. Cultural intelligence is an individual difference, but unlike personality, which is relatively enduring, it is considered to be something that can be developed and enhanced through interventions that organisations can make. It has four components:

1 Mind (meta-cognitions): learning strategies, whereby people can acquire and develop coping strategies. Individuals need to identify a 'point of entry' into a foreign culture – for example, a form of behaviour or a context that can be used subsequently to interpret different patterns of behaviour.

RESOURCING THROUGH INTERNATIONAL MANAGEMENT TEAMS

There are a number of reasons why international management teams have become more important:

❖ Strategies of rapid internationalisation through International joint ventures, strategic partnership arrangements, and global start-ups all place international employees into team and work contexts where they have less direct personal position power, but do have a heightened need to ensure that there is learning from the partnership.

❖ Globalisation of operations is pushing the requirement for international working lower down the hierarchy.

There are many examples of how such teams are used. They may be part of an international supply chain, or a cross-national team of consultants used to deliver a business solution, or an international relief team for a not-for-profit organisation. Whatever their purpose, these transnational teams of managers and specialists need to be resourced in ways that ensure that the talents of people in the team have been carefully blended to make sound decisions. It has been argued that transnational teams contribute a very important 'glue technology' in international organisations — they represent a process technology that is used as a co-ordination mechanism within those organisations. In order to be effective, they have to be founded on effective relationships between and within teams, because such teams have to:

❖ encourage cohesiveness among national and functional units

❖ create lateral networks to improve communication and information flow between subsidiaries and HQ, and among subsidiaries

❖ provide opportunities for team members to understand issues better and note the interdependencies between units

❖ provide opportunities to learn how to function more effectively within different cultures, suppliers, customers and employees

❖ foster knowledge transfer and organisational learning.[29]

---

2   Knowledge about different cultures (cognition).

3   Heart (emotional/motivational): people need to have the desire to persevere in the face of challenge when adapting to a new culture, and a belief in their own ability to master a situation (called self-efficacy).

4   Body (physical behaviour): people need to develop a repertoire of culturally appropriate behaviours. This centres around the ability to mirror customs and gestures, and adopt habits and mannerisms, in order to enter the world of a foreign culture and enable the development of trust.

Rather than the progressive stages of trans-cultural competence, an individual may be seen to be strong in some of these areas, weaker in others. Based on survey data from 2,000 managers from 60 cultures, 6 typical combinations were identified (such as provincial, analyst, mimic, natural, ambassador), the ultimate being a chameleon, with strengths in all areas.

INTERNATIONAL MANAGEMENT TEAMS

Given the problems associated with the management of expatriates and their relevance to an international resourcing strategy, in many organisations it is cross-boundary teams, rather than expatriates, that are now to be considered as the basic unit of the global economy.

It is therefore essential for HR professionals to develop policies and practices that support the use of teams, including selecting team players, rewarding teamwork and developing mentoring and coaching behaviours for potential team leaders. Research on the productivity of international teams shows that they can be far more effective than mono-cultural teams, but if poorly managed they can also be far less effective.[30]

There are many reasons why diversity can lead to lower effectiveness. Diversity makes sense-making, trust and decision-making more difficult because stereotyping takes over from accurate assessment; misperception, mis-interpretation, mis-evaluation and miscommunication abound; stress levels increase; and much information is seen as inappropriate. Groups are therefore initially less cohesive.[31] Members of international teams need to understand: what is the behaviour? Why is the behaviour considered desirable? At whom is the behaviour aimed? Where is the behaviour most often seen? How is the behaviour delivered?

In short, even where organisations are pursuing resourcing strategies that avoid the need for international recruitment, such as reliance on international teams, they need to think about the skills implications almost as much as if they are recruiting a cadre of specialist expatriates.

Based on a range of research that has looked at the nature of cross-cultural communication, the competency specification

Table 1 ❖ Cross-cultural communication competence[32]			
Interpersonal skills	**Team effectiveness**	**Cultural uncertainty**	**Cultural empathy**
❖ Ability to acknowledge differences in communication and interaction styles	❖ Ability to understand and define team goals, roles and norms	❖ Ability to deal with cultural uncertainty	❖ Ability to see and understand the world from others' cultural perspectives
❖ Ability to deal with misunderstandings	❖ Ability to give and receive constructive feedback	❖ Ability to display patience	❖ Exhibiting a spirit of inquiry about other cultures, values, beliefs and communication patterns
❖ Comfort when communicating with foreign nationals	❖ Ability to discuss and solve problems	❖ Tolerance of ambiguity and uncertainty due to cultural differences	
❖ Awareness of one's own cultural conditioning	❖ Ability to deal with conflict situations	❖ Openness to cultural differences	❖ Ability to appreciate dissimilar working styles
❖ Basic knowledge about the country, the culture, and the language of team members	❖ Ability to display respect for other team members	❖ Ability to exercise flexibility	❖ Ability to accept different ways of doing things
	❖ Participatory leadership style		❖ Non-judgemental stance toward the ways things are done in other situations
	❖ Ability to work co-operatively with others		

shown in Table 1, above, has been developed for effective operation in international teams.

INTERNATIONAL COMMUTERS AND FREQUENT FLYERS

Another development that lessens the need for additional international recruitment – but indirectly adds an additional international role requirement and expectation to existing jobs – is the growth of flexible international travel. Since the mid-1990s a variety of reports has generally evidenced greater use of alternative forms of assignment relative to reliance on long-term assignments. These include short-term 'commuter' or 'rotator' assignments (where individuals fly back and forth to work in another country at regular intervals) and 'frequent flyers' (where individuals simply conduct business on the basis of frequent visits).[33] Other alternatives include localisation strategies and one-way moves. However, it can sometimes be a false economy to assume that these alternatives are cheaper than long-term expatriation. In addition to the personal stress and dissatisfaction and complex tax administration, they may not even be monitored or evaluated by HR departments.

> '...it can sometimes be a false economy to assume that these alternatives are cheaper than long-term expatriation.'

The example in the box opposite provides some estimates of the increasing levels of international mobility within jobs.

It is also easy to assume that staff who do not operate as full-time

expatriates but work instead as (for example) frequent commuters do not need specific skills for international operation. However, research at CReME found that in addition to problems of long work hours, social and family separation, this type of international employee still reports that they suffer from a lack of cultural integration.[34] The competencies listed in Table 1 have relevance to this group, too. Experts point out that care and attention is needed because:[35]

❖ there is often a wish by the organisation to provide management development, and the informal selection process can work against this

❖ the work that they do often requires rapid integration into international work groups, actually increasing their need for cross-cultural skills

❖ in many instances these individuals move on from a self-initiated foreign assignment to become career international managers, moving into these roles by default rather than through any traditional selection considerations.

SELF-INITIATED MOVERS AND IMMIGRANTS

For many UK organisations, rather than relying on the use of expatriates there is now an opportunity to attract a category of employees called self-initiated foreign assignments,[36] or more euphemistically SIM-patriates (standing for Self-Initiated Movers). Many industrial sectors have learned how to capitalise on the fact that some cities become a magnet for such self-initiated movers, and therefore a useful source for international recruitment. Yet very little is known about this group of international employee.[37]

IS INTERNATIONAL MOBILITY ON THE INCREASE?

The Barclaycard Business Travel Survey drew upon data from a sample of 2,500 senior manager respondents taken from the population of 565,000 business card holders.

❖ With long-haul travel increasing, the number of flights taken per business traveller will increase by 12%, from 7.6 flights per year in 2005/6 to 8.5 flights in 2015.

❖ Low-cost air travel is predicted to be near saturation point and will therefore level off, with 74% of business travellers expected to use these services in 2015.

❖ Nearly half (45%) of business travellers say they are travelling for business more in 2005/6 than they were in 2004/5.

❖ In contrast, actual miles travelled per month have decreased from 642 in 2004/5 to 608.5 in 2005/6. The main reason given for the increase in business travel is business expansion, both overseas (33%) and in the UK (18%).

❖ Of those who say they are travelling less, 25% put this down to technology reducing the need.

❖ Total distance travelled per week will increase to approximately 700 miles per person, compared to 609 miles currently.

❖ Business people will on average spend an extra night away from home each month, up from 4.1 nights in 2005/6 to 5.2 nights in 2015.

❖ Trade in the UK is already becoming more global, affected not only by countries such as Poland joining the EU but also by the opening-up of economies, such as China's.

❖ The top business destinations over the last twelve months were: UK and Ireland (75%); Western Europe (56%); USA and Canada (23%); Asia Pacific (10%); Eastern Europe (10%); China (7%); and Africa (4%).

For example, a sample of university-educated Finnish employees on foreign assignments indicated that about one-third of them had found jobs for themselves whilst abroad.[38] The background of these employees was diverse, covering all age groups and people with very different motives for going abroad. The organisations that employed them were not always multinationals but were often domestic organisations seeking people with international experience to work in their domestic operations.

It might be argued that organisations do not need to worry too much about the skills and competencies (and therefore selection) of these individuals. Their availability just helps solve an immediate resourcing pressure in a particular project. International competencies can then be built by recruiting young, high-potential employees to challenging tasks or projects in a home or third country: the job gets done and it is hoped that international competencies are built at the same time. In many instances, however, these individuals are chosen for specific project reasons, or they select themselves. However, some of the cautions noted above in relation to international commuters apply to this group as well.

In recent years a number of centres have become 'magnets' for these self-initiated movers. For example, Dublin has become a centre of international operations for many service functions or organisations, as the example of Teleservices in the box on page 16 shows, and this had been fuelled by an influx of international movers. The same can of course be said of the City of London, which has become a broker location for many individuals wishing to pursue a more international career.

> '...Dublin has become a centre of international operations for many service functions or organisations...'

An area of fruitful recent research on the skills and competencies that are important for international employees has been work by psychologists on people who learn to transfer across cultures and absorb new cultures – ie, integrated migrants. Rather than just rely on knowledge about expatriates and global leaders, it is argued that organisations – as a consequence of their international resourcing policies – face a new context of *intra-cultural diversity*. This is true both within societies but also within the sorts of situation outlined overleaf for organisations operating in Dublin.

What do we know about the skills and competencies that are important for successful 'within-culture functioning'? Organisations that are recruiting these different types of international employee can find that they are particularly effective at the modelling skills mentioned in Figure 1. This context requires people to learn by observation, enabling them to acquire knowledge, attitudes, values, emotional proclivities and

NEW MODELS FOR SOURCES OF GLOBAL LABOUR: THE CITY OF DUBLIN

The Teleservices Forum of Ireland reports that the last 10 years have seen massive growth in this sector. By 2000 there were already 60 call centres in Ireland, of which 50 were multilingual, employing 6,000 people. By this time, jobs in international teleservices usually required a high level of fluency in one or more Continental European languages, and up to one-third of employees in Irish call centres were non-Irish nationals employed for their language proficiency.[39]

Irish Development Agency promotional literature placed employment costs in Ireland below France, the UK, Netherlands, Germany and Belgium for telesales staff, and annual hours worked above these countries. Coupled with a young and educated workforce, modern telecommunications infrastructure and incentives for multinational investment, it has made Dublin a vibrant international labour market.

However, the whole population of Ireland is little more than that of the city of Berlin, and the rapidly evolving labour market dictates a specific operating model. Originally there was no shortage of Irish graduates who had foreign languages, but this labour market has long since dried up, and most firms now rely on a different resourcing model. Since May 2004, 2,000 citizens from the new EU accession countries travel to Ireland every week to live and work, on either a temporary or permanent basis. The Irish Business and Employers Confederation[40] and other partners have recently completed the Interact project, which is aimed at supporting employers with multicultural workplaces.[41]

competencies through the information that is conveyed. They develop three important 'agency skills':[42]

❖ direct personal agency to manage their own lives and bring influence to bear directly on themselves and their own environment

❖ proxy agency skills for those spheres of people's lives where they have no direct control over the social and institutional practices that affect everyday life, and so rely on others – and must influence others – to act on their behalf and secure personally desired outcomes, that is, socially interdependent effort

❖ collective agency skills, where people act in concert with others to shape their future by pooling knowledge, skills and resources, forming alliances, and acting in mutual support to secure that which they cannot accomplish on their own.

This type of research will have some clear practical benefits – for personnel selection systems for expatriates and other forms of international employees – but especially in the context of HR functions needing more culturally diverse workforces, even in their domestic markets, because of new forms of international working.

We therefore continue by looking at one of the driving forces behind the need for more international recruitment: the skills shortages in the UK market, the increases in international migration and the changing regulatory environment within which international recruitment is taking place.

ENDNOTES

1 Sparrow, P.R. (1999) International recruitment, selection and assessment: whose route map will you follow? In P. Joynt and B. Morton (eds) *The Global HR manager: creating the seamless organisation*. London: IPD.

2 Baruch, Y. and Altman, Y. (2002) Expatriation and repatriation in MNCs: a taxonomy. *Human Resource Management*. Vol. 41, No. 2. 239–59.

3 Pucik, V. (1998) Selecting and developing the global versus the expatriate manager: a review of the state of the art. *Human Resource Planning*. Vol. 21, No.4. 40–54, p.41.

4 Welch, D.E. (2003) Globalisation of staff movements: beyond cultural adjustment. *Management International Review*. Vol. 43, No. 2. 149–69.

5 Yamazaki, Y. and Kayes, C. (2004) An experiential approach to cross-cultural learning: a review and integration of competencies for successful expatriate adaptation. *Academy of Management Learning and Education*. Vol. 5, No. 4. 362–79.

6 Spreitzer, G.M., McCall, M.W. and Mahoney, J.D. (1997) Early identification of international executive potential. *Journal of Applied Psychology*. Vol. 82, No. 1. 6–29.

7 This is based on an amalgam of reviews by Stroh, L.K., Black, J.S., Mendenhall, M.E. and Gregersen, H.B. (2005) *International assignments: an integration of strategy, research and practice*. London: Lawrence Erlbaum; Yamazaki, Y. and Kayes, C. (2004) An experiential approach to cross-cultural learning: a review and integration of competencies for successful expatriate adaptation. *Academy of Management Learning and Education*. Vol. 5, No. 4. 362–79; Pucik, V. (1998) Selecting and developing the global versus the expatriate manager: a review of the state of the art. *Human Resource Planning*. Vol. 21, No. 4. 40–54, Aycan, Z. (1997) Expatriate adjustment as a multifaceted phenomenon: Individual and organisational level predictors. *The International Journal of Human Resource Management*. Vol. 8, No. 4. 434–56. These in turn have drawn upon early work by Dinges, N.G. and Baldwin, K.D. (1996) Intercultural competence: a research perspective. In D. Landis and R.S. Bhagat (eds) *Handbook of intercultural training*. Thousand Oaks, CA: Sage; Mendenhall, M.E. and Oddou, G.R. (1985) The dimensions of expatriate acculturation: a review. *Academy of Management Review*. Vol. 10. 39–47; Tung, R.L. (1981) Selection and Training of personnel overseas assignments, *Columbia Journal of World Business*. Vol. 16, No.1. 68–78.

8 Mendenhall, M.E., Kühlman, T.M., Stahl, G. and Osland, J.S. (2002) Employee development and expatriate assignts, In M.J. Gannon and K.L. Newman (eds) *Handbook of cross-cultural management*. London: Blackwell.

9 Black, J.S., Mendenhall, M., and Oddou, G. (1991) Towards a comprehensive model of international adjustment: an integration of multiple theoretical perspectives. *Academy of Management Review.* Vol. 16. 291–317.

10 Aycan, Z. (1997) Expatriate adjustment as a multifaceted phenomenon: Individual and organisational level predictors. *The International Journal of Human Resource Management,* Vol. 8, No. 4. 434–56.

11 Adler, N.J. (1983) Cross-cultural management research: the ostrich and the trend. *Academy of Management Review.* Vol. 8. 226–32.

12 Osland, J. (1995) *The adventure of working abroad: hero tales from the global frontier.* San Francisco, CA: Jossey-Bass.

13 Kealey, D.J. (1996) The challenge of international personnel selection. In D. Landis and R.S. Bhagat (eds) *Handbook of intercultural training.* 2nd edn, pp. 80–105. Thousand Oaks: Sage.

14 Stahl, G.K. (1998) *Internationaler Einsatz von Fuhrungskräften.* Munich: Oldenbourg.

15 Leiba-O'Sullivan, S. (1999) The distinction between stable and dynamic cross-cultural competencies: implications for expatriate trainability. *Journal of International Business Systems.* Vol. 30, No 4 709–25.

16 Bhaskar-Shrinivas, P., Harrison, D.A., Shaffer, M.A. and Luk, D.M. (2005) Input-based and time-based models of international adjustment: meta-analytic evidence and theoretical extensions. *Academy of Management Journal.* Vol. 48, No. 2. 257–81.

17 Worldlink (2005) Expats' partners: professionals working to get permit constraints relaxed. *Worldlink.* Vol.15, No. 2. 2–3.

18 GMAC Global relocation Services (2005) *Global relocation Trends 2005 Survey Report.* Woodridge, IL: GMAC.

19 Hempel, G. (2005) Renaisaance of the GEC: the what, the why and the when. *Worldlink.* Vol. 15, No. 3. 4–5.

20 Morrison, A.J. (2000) Developing a global leadership model, *Human Resource Management.* Vol. 39, Nos. 2/3. 117–31, p.119.

21 Harvard Business Review (2003) Perspectives: In search of global leaders. *Harvard Business Review,* August: 38–45.

22 Bartlett, C.A. and Ghoshal, S. (1989) *Managing across borders: the transnational solution.* Boston, MA: Harvard Business School Press, p.195.

23 Murtha, T.P., Lenway, S.A. and Bagozzi, R.P. (1998) Global mind-sets and cognitive shift in a complex multinational corporation, *Strategic Management Journal.* Vol. 19. 97–114.

24 See for example: Bonache, J. and Brewster, C. (2001) Knowledge transfer and the management of expatriation, *Thunderbird International Business Review.* Vol. 43, No. 1. 145–68; Cerdin, J.-L. (2003) International diffusion of HRM practices: the role of expatriates, *Beta: Scandinavian Journal of Business Research.* Vol. 17, No. 1. 48–58; Athanassiou, N. and Nigh, D. (1999) The impact of company internationalisation on top management team advice networks: a tacit knowledge perspective. *Strategic Management Journal.* Vol. 19, No. 1. 83–92; Makela, A.K. (2004) The social capital of expatriates and

repatriates: knowledge sharing through interpersonal cross-border relationships. *Paper presented at EIASM Workshop on Expatriation, Brussels,* 18–19 October; Smale, A. and Riusala, K. (2004) Predicting stickiness factors in the international transfer of knowledge through expatriates. *Paper presented at EIASM Workshop on Expatriation, Brussels,* 18–19 October.

25 For details see: Ashkanasy, N.M., Trevor-Roberts, E. and Earnshaw, L. (2002) The Anglo Cluster: legacy of the British empire, *Journal of World Business.* Vol. 37. 28–39; House, R.J. et al (2004) *Culture, Leadership and Organisation: a GLOBE study of 62 societies.* Thousand Oaks, CA: Sage; House, R.J., Hanges, P.J., Ruiz-Quintanilla, S.A., Dorfman, P.W., Javidan, M., Dickson, M., Gupta, V. and GLOBE (1999) Cultural influences on leadership and organisations: project GLOBE. In W. F. Mobley, M.J. Gessner and V. Arnold (eds) *Advances in global leadership, volume 1,* Stanford, CT: JAI Press. 171–233; House, R.J., Javidan, M., Hanges, P. and Dorfman, P. (2002) Understanding cultures and implicit leadership theories across the globe: an introduction to project GLOBE, *Journal of World Business.* Vol. 37. 3–10.

26 Harvey, M., and Novicevic, M.M. (2004) The development of political skill and political capital by global leaders through global assignments. *International Journal of Human Resource Management.* Vol. 15, No. 7. 1173–188, p.1173.

27 Zimmermann, A. and Sparrow, P.R. (in press – 2006) Mutual adjustment processes in international teams: lessons for the study of expatriation. *International Studies in Management and Organisation.*

28 See Farley, P.C. and Ang, S. (2003) *Cultural intelligence: individual interactions across cultures.* Stanford, CA: Stanford University Press; and Earley, P.C. and Mosakowski, E. (2004) Cultural intelligence, *Harvard Business Review.* 139 46; and Ng, K.-Y. and Earley, P.C. (2006) Old constructs, new frontiers, *Group & Organization Management.* Vol. 31, No. 1. 4–19.

29 Schneider, S.C. and Barsoux, J.L. (1997) The multicultural team, in *Managing across cultures,* Hemel Hempstead: Prentice Hall

30 Shapiro, D.L., Furst, S.A., Spreitzer, G.M. and Von Glinow, M.A. (2002) Transnational teams in the electronic age: are team identity and high performance at risk? *Journal of Organisational Behavior.* Vol. 23. 455–67.

31 Ilgen, D., LePine, J. and Hollenbeck, J. (1999) Effective decision making in multinational teams. In P.C. Earley and M. Erez (eds) *New approaches to intercultural and international industrial/ organisational psychology.* San Francisco: New Lexington Press. 377–409.

32 Matveev, A.V. and Nelson, P.E. (2004) Cross cultural communication competence and multicultural team performance: perceptions of American and Russian managers. *International Journal of Cross Cultural Management.* Vol. 4, No. 2. 253–70.

33 Johnson, R. (2003) Final destination. *People Management.* Vol. 9, No. 2. 40–43.

34 Johnson, R. (2003) Final destination. *People Management.* Vol. 9, No. 2. 40–43.

35 Tahvanainen, M. and Worm, V. (2004) Short-term international assignments: how do companies manage them? *Paper presented at EIASM Workshop on Expatriation,* Brussels, 18–19 October.

36 Inkson, K., Arthur, M.B., Pringle, J. and Barry, S. (1997) Expatriate assignment versus overseas experience: contrasting models of international human resource development. *Journal of World Business.* Vol. 32, No. 4. 351–68.

37 Bonache, J., Brewster, C. and Suutari, V. (2001) Expatriation: a developing research agenda. *Thunderbird International Business Review*. Vol. 43, No. 1. 3–20.

38 Suutari, V. and Brewster, C. (2000) Making their own way: international experience through self-initiated foreign assignments. *Journal of World Business*.

39 Byrne, A. (2000) Call centre sector will grow. *Irish Times*, October. Website: http:// www.skoool.ie/skoool/careermatters.asp?id=857

40 Irish Business and Employers Confederation (2005) *IBEC Annual Review 04/05*. Dublin: IBEC.

41 Redmond, D. and Butler, P. (2003) *Promoting an intercultural workplace: building on diversity. Report on the experience of Irish and migrant workers.* October 2003 Dublin: Nexus Research Co-operative.

42 See: Bandura, A. (2001) Social cognitive theory: an agentic perspective. *Annual review of psychology, volume 52.* Palo Alto: Annual Reviews Inc. 1–26; Bandura, A. (2002) Social cognitive theory in cultural context. *Applied Psychology: An International Review.* Vol. 51, No. 2. 269–90, p.270.

INTERNATIONAL MIGRATION AND THE IMPACT ON RECRUITMENT

* ❖ **Dramatic increase in labour movement within the EU**

* ❖ **Migrant workers offer advantages**

* ❖ **Increasing supply of and need for migrant workers**

It is not just changes in expatriate mobility that vex international recruiters. The most significant shift by far has been the emergence of much higher levels of international labour mobility in general. This development has in fact reduced the need for many organisations to rely on a specialised cadre of international employees. The UK population, and consequently the labour market, has become highly internationalised. OECD data show that the annual inflow of long-term foreign workers into the UK increased from 9,900 in 1992 to 50,300 by 2001, more than doubling from 1999 to 2001 alone.[1]

Traditionally the level of mobility within the EU has actually been very low – before the incorporation of the new accession countries, fewer than 0.5 per cent of Europe's 350 million citizens had moved from one member state to another.[2] For example, there are 195,000 French nationals – 10 per cent of all the overseas French – working in the UK. Since 2001 there has been further rapid expansion of international migration, due both to supply and demand factors.

> 'Since 2001 there has been...rapid expansion of international migration...'

In terms of demand, employers feel that a migrant workforce can provide not just the necessary skills, but high levels of dependability and commitment. A recent Home Office study[3] shows that migrant workers from Eastern Europe have in some instances become a preferred source of labour because of their work ethic and skills, particularly in the agricultural and hotel and catering industries, and for low-skilled administrative, business and management jobs. Recruited migrants are both high-skill and low-skill, typically students or in their twenties or thirties. The risk with this development of course is that domestic organisations might be tempted not to invest in training in their home markets but use international recruitment as a short-term strategy to harness superior skills from overseas.

BORN ABROAD STUDY

Recently the Born Abroad study[4] examined: data from the 2001 census against previous censuses to establish the geographical location of the immigrant population; data from the Labour Force Survey to compare the age, gender, employment status, earnings and education levels of new immigrants; and data taken from the Office of National Statistics (ONS), International Passenger Survey (IPS) and Home Office immigration statistics to map broad immigration trends. It presents a comprehensive picture of Britain's new immigrant communities – defined as those who have arrived since 1990 – from over 50 countries and regions.

It established that the proportion of people living in Britain born abroad – that is, outside the British Isles – has increased from 4.6 to 7.5% since 1971. From 1991–2001 this population grew by 36%. Indians and Pakistanis make up the largest immigrant communities, followed by those born in Germany, the Caribbean and the USA. The last 15 years have seen a rapid growth in communities from non-traditional immigration countries. The number of immigrants from the former Yugoslavia has tripled. Those from Sierra Leone, China, South Africa and Sweden have doubled. The Caribbean-born community declined by over 12,000 between 1991 and 2001. Forty-one per cent of immigrants are based in London, making up 25% of the capital's population. In 2004, 62% of new immigrants were in employment, compared with only 49% in 1994. This varies markedly across source country. The new immigrant communities with the highest levels of employment come from New Zealand (93.6%), Australia (90.6%) and the Philippines (85.4%). The

INTERNATIONAL MIGRATION AND THE IMPACT ON RECRUITMENT

❖ **Dramatic increase in labour movement within the EU**

❖ **Migrant workers offer advantages**

❖ **Increasing supply of and need for migrant workers**

It is not just changes in expatriate mobility that vex international recruiters. The most significant shift by far has been the emergence of much higher levels of international labour mobility in general. This development has in fact reduced the need for many organisations to rely on a specialised cadre of international employees. The UK population, and consequently the labour market, has become highly internationalised. OECD data show that the annual inflow of long-term foreign workers into the UK increased from 9,900 in 1992 to 50,300 by 2001, more than doubling from 1999 to 2001 alone.[1]

Traditionally the level of mobility within the EU has actually been very low – before the incorporation of the new accession countries, fewer than 0.5 per cent of Europe's 350 million citizens had moved from one member state to another.[2] For example, there are 195,000 French nationals – 10 per cent of all the overseas French working in the UK. Since 2001 there has been further rapid expansion of international migration, due both to supply and demand factors.

> 'Since 2001 there has been...rapid expansion of international migration...'

In terms of demand, employers feel that a migrant workforce can provide not just the necessary skills, but high levels of dependability and commitment. A recent Home Office study[3] shows that migrant workers from Eastern Europe have in some instances become a preferred source of labour because of their work ethic and skills, particularly in the agricultural and hotel and catering industries, and for low-skilled administrative, business and management jobs. Recruited migrants are both high-skill and low-skill, typically students or in their twenties or thirties. The risk with this development of course is that domestic organisations might be tempted not to invest in training in their home markets but use international recruitment as a short-term strategy to harness superior skills from overseas.

BORN ABROAD STUDY

Recently the Born Abroad study[4] examined: data from the 2001 census against previous censuses to establish the geographical location of the immigrant population; data from the Labour Force Survey to compare the age, gender, employment status, earnings and education levels of new immigrants; and data taken from the Office of National Statistics (ONS), International Passenger Survey (IPS) and Home Office immigration statistics to map broad immigration trends. It presents a comprehensive picture of Britain's new immigrant communities – defined as those who have arrived since 1990 – from over 50 countries and regions.

It established that the proportion of people living in Britain born abroad – that is, outside the British Isles – has increased from 4.6 to 7.5% since 1971. From 1991–2001 this population grew by 36%. Indians and Pakistanis make up the largest immigrant communities, followed by those born in Germany, the Caribbean and the USA. The last 15 years have seen a rapid growth in communities from non-traditional immigration countries. The number of immigrants from the former Yugoslavia has tripled. Those from Sierra Leone, China, South Africa and Sweden have doubled. The Caribbean-born community declined by over 12,000 between 1991 and 2001. Forty-one per cent of immigrants are based in London, making up 25% of the capital's population. In 2004, 62% of new immigrants were in employment, compared with only 49% in 1994. This varies markedly across source country. The new immigrant communities with the highest levels of employment come from New Zealand (93.6%), Australia (90.6%) and the Philippines (85.4%). The lowest employment levels come from Somalia (12.2%), Angola (30%) and Iran (31.7%). A significant proportion of recent immigrants are highly qualified. For example, 37% of new immigrants in Scotland hold a higher-level qualification, the highest of any region.

However, supply has also increased. Applications to the Highly Skilled Migrant Programme introduced in January 2002 have increased from 150 to 500 a week in the last two years. In May and June 2004, workers from the new EU accession states accepted under the UK Worker Registration Scheme were estimated to have contributed £4 million a week to the UK's GDP. In the UK university sector, overseas appointments represented 29% of all new hires in 2003–04. A *Times Higher Education Supplement* survey of the top 16 universities found that, for the period 2003–05, this figure had risen to 35%, rising to 46% and 48% for Imperial College and Oxford University.[5] The figures were highest for young, talented researchers.

EXPERIENCE FROM THE CONSTRUCTION SECTOR

Some sectors – for example, construction or hotels, catering and leisure – now operate in a highly internationalised labour market. In its submission to the Home Office on Making Migration Work for Britain, the Sector Skills Council for construction pointed out that the sector accounts for 8% of UK GDP and employment.[6] As an industry it has witnessed an increase in the use of migrant labour, primarily to plug skills gaps. This process has been intensified by the expansion of the EU.

The industry needs to recruit and train some 88,000 entrants per year over the next five years, with 21,000 in the four main trades, 14,000 specialists and civil engineering occupations, 11,000 in managerial and supervisory roles, 8,000 in professional and technical roles and 14,000 in electrical, plumbing and related trades. Currently, non-UK citizens account for about 3% of the total current industry workforce (5% among the largest firms employing 250 or more across the UK). A recent CITB-Construction Skills study[7] showed that, currently, 7% of employers (excluding the self-employed) had employed non-UK citizens in the previous six months.

However, historical failures to invest in UK skills will probably result in a greater need for international migration to fill skills gaps and shortages. Thirty-one per cent of companies employing non-UK citizens expect the proportion of non-UK employees to grow. As a consequence of such skills demands, firms in the sector need to:

❖ integrate a multi-language workforce

❖ cope with health and safety issues

❖ cope with the need to ensure comparability of qualifications

❖ ensure English language requirements are met by migrant workers to aid safe working conditions

❖ ensure that inward migration does not occur to the detriment of domestic employment and productivity levels.

In line with these trends, data show that international recruitment both of professional employees and craft skill groups has increased markedly in recent years. The CIPD Quarterly HR Trends and Indicators survey showed that, by the end of 2004, 28% of employers would be recruiting from abroad, rising to nearly 40% of firms that employ more than 500 employees.[8]

The CIPD's 2005 Annual Recruitment, Retention and Turnover survey showed that 38% of firms were recruiting from abroad – up to 44% in public services. Of those now recruiting overseas, 53% expected this activity to increase.[9] This is a particular issue for firms either in London or in the public sector and is primarily the result of a greater number of vacancies and skills shortages.

WHERE CAN I FIND OUT MORE?

Research or reports on a range of important issues are made available through the Social Science Information Gateway (SOSIG) (http://www.sosig.ac.uk). This provides a trusted source of selected, high-quality Internet information for researchers and professionals in the social sciences, business and law. For example, reports can be found on knowledge worker migration, labour market performance of immigrants, international trends in migration and foreign worker in-flows. SOSIG is hosted by the Institute of Learning and Research Technology at the University of Bristol. It receives funding from the UK Economic and Social Research Council (ESRC) and the UK Joint Information Systems Committee (JISC). The catalogue points to thousands of resources, and each one has been selected and described by a librarian or academic and is supported by a database of over 250,000 social science webpages. Whereas the resources found in the SOSIG Internet Catalogue have been selected by subject experts, those in the Social Science Search Engine have been collected by software called a 'harvester' (similar mechanisms may be referred to as 'robots' or 'web crawlers'). All the pages collected stem from the main Internet catalogue; this provides the equivalent of a social science search engine.

ENDNOTES

1   Data taken from OECD sources: *Trends in International Migration*.

2   Hong, V. (2001) Europe learns to hire on the wire. *Industry Standard Europe*. 15 March. 66–7.

3   Dench, S., Hurstfield, J., Hill, D. and Akroyd, K. (2006) *Employers' use of migrant labour: summary report*. Home Office Report 03/06. Institute for Employment Studies.

4   Kyambi, S. (2005) *Beyond black and white: mapping new immigrant communities*. Institute for Public Policy Research. Details available on www.bbc.co.uk/bornabroad

5   Wainwright, T. (2005) UK looks abroad to fill jobs. *Times Higher Education Supplement*. No. 1702, 29 July. 1.

6   I am grateful to both Guy Hazlehurst. Deputy Director, Skills Strategy and Lee Bryer – Research Analyst at CITB-Construction Skills for providing access to research on Workforce Mobility and Skills in the UK Construction Sector, which was designed to provide reliable data on the nature of the construction workforce in the UK in regard to their qualification levels and the extent of occupational and geographic mobility within the workforce, and to the response to the Home Office Consultation Selective Admission: Making Migration Work for Britain, which provides further additional commentary on the current skills issues related to migration of workers into our sector.

7   IFF Research, Employer attitudes and motivations to learning and training, 2005 (*Unpublished*)

8   Czerny, A. (2004) UK's foreign trawl continues. *People Management*. Vol. 10, No. 20. 7.

9   CIPD (2005) *Recruitment, retention and turnover annual survey report*. London: CIPD.

CHANGES IN IMMIGRATION POLICY AND VISA ARRANGEMENTS **3**

- ❖ **Migrant workers add value to the UK economy**

- ❖ **The UK is moving towards a points system**

- ❖ **Immigration rules are already changing**

The government sees migration as necessary in supporting sustainable economic growth and addressing skill shortages. It has embarked on a process of 'managed migration', which, in addition to a package of legislative changes, also involves building public understanding of this need and consultation with employers and trade unions about migration policies. Support for this process has been expressed by the Home Office, CBI (Confederation of British Industry) and Trades Union Congress (TUC), who released a joint statement in September 2005 agreeing that this is in the interests of the UK economy. They believe that the contribution made by overseas workers must be recognised and enhanced.

> '...the contribution made by overseas workers must be recognised and enhanced.'

CHANGES IN POLICY AND THE NEW POINTS SYSTEM

The UK Government has established a five-year plan to shift the entire UK work permit system for migrants to one based on points. It will soon be releasing details of the reforms to the visa system proposed in the Immigration, Asylum and Nationality Bill. The Bill proposes replacing the current system for asylum with a single points system. Currently there are different work permits and entry schemes for different categories, such as employees, students and immigrants. Firm proposals for the new system and a timetable for implementation were expected in spring 2006. The intention is to create a system that attracts skilled labour in job areas such as engineering, the financial sector, education and the health service. Officially the intention is not to increase or reduce the number of people coming to the UK, but to ensure that the UK takes only as many people as the economy needs at any one time and that those who come are selected. The basic principle is one of 'entry-through-skills'. The more skills you have, the more points you will gain, and the more likelihood of entry to the UK. European Union workers and workers from a few other European countries will not be affected and will still be able to come and go under the free market rules also available to British people. Similar systems are already used in other industrialised countries, such as Australia and the USA, where it is believed that points systems are more transparent and responsive to the needs of the economy.[1]

The proposed new points system consists of five categories of worker entry into the UK in four tiers:

Tier 1 – Highly skilled: for example, doctors, engineers, IT specialists and top graduates in key sectors such as business and finance. As the most skilled professionals they will automatically have enough points to come to the UK without a job offer and seek work or set up a business. Workers in this category will have the most flexibility in the UK and the greatest opportunities to settle for good.

Tier 2 – Skilled: for instance, people with qualifications or important work-related experience in a wide range of sectors from health service workers to white-collar jobs and the trades. Points will be given on the basis of talents. They will be allowed into the UK if they have a job offer in a 'shortage area'.

Tier 3 – Low skilled: currently, temporary migration from all over the world is allowed to jobs in hospitality, food processing and agriculture. These permissions will be phased out in favour of workers from the expanded European Union, although there may be controlled quotas in certain sectors. Workers in this category must find an employer as a sponsor, and the employer will have some responsibility for ensuring the migrant remains within the terms of his or her visa.

Tier 4 – Specialists and students: these might be students paying for tuition in the UK or foreign government representatives, and possibly professional sports people and ministers of religion. This tier applies to those where there is 'no significant issue of competition' but an economic benefit resulting from someone's presence.

Only workers in the top two tiers will be allowed to seek permanent residence in the UK, and the period leading to permanent residence will be increased from four to five years. The Home Office will have the final say about shortage areas but will establish an independent advisory board – the Skills Advisory Body – to provide accurate information on where gaps exist. For example, if in one year there is a shortage of plumbers in the UK, this board might recommend awarding more entry points to foreign plumbers, but once the gap is plugged, a few months later it might suggest cutting the points available.

Currently, individuals granted a permit to work in the UK might have to wait four years before being able to win indefinite leave to remain. Although under the new proposals this period would rise to five years, some migrants from the top two categories of sought-after immigrants (professionals, entrepreneurs and skilled workers) could be granted leave 'much earlier', although no time-scale has yet been disclosed.

Workers in some sectors 'prone to abuse' will be required to hand over a financial bond, repayable when they leave at the end of their visa. Employers would also be fined £2,000 for each illegal worker.

In relation to the current developments in policy, there have been a number of recent changes in regulations that affect international recruitment:[2]

❖ Since May 2004, nationals of new EU member states, except Malta and Cyprus, wishing to work in the UK for more than a month have been required to register under the Worker Registration Scheme. Once a person has been working legally in the UK for 12 months without a break, they have full rights of free movement and are no longer required to register under this scheme. From 1 October 2005 the fee for registering under the scheme rose from £50 to £70.

❖ Previously, people who had been seconded overseas during the previous 12 months, but whose salary continued to be paid in another country, were assessed against the country where they actually worked. However, as from 8 September 2005, the UK Home Office has changed this rule. Applications from individuals who have been seconded overseas and have claimed points for past earnings will be considered against the income band of the country in which their position is normally held. Applicants for the Highly Skilled Migrant Programme can claim up to a maximum of 50 points for their earnings during the 12-month period prior to the application being made.

❖ The Home Office has required new applicants for British Citizenship from 1 November 2005 to demonstrate knowledge both of the English language and life in the UK. Applicants whose ability in English is at or above the standard

of English for Speakers of Other Languages (ESOL) Entry Level 3 will be able to take a short test on a computer at a series of UK test centres. Applicants below this level must complete new ESOL citizenship classes.

There are differing opinions about the desirability of such a system, as well as some practical issues that it can create for international recruitment, selection and assessment. For example, there are fears in some sectors that it might inadvertently damage overseas recruitment. Universities have expressed concern over the intention to abandon the appeals system.[3] The government argues that a points system would be robust enough to avoid the need for appeals, although at present it is not known how the points system will work, how points will be allocated and what weightings will be applied to which entry criteria.

> 'The CBI...has concerns that...employers...are expected to act as immigration officials.'

Universities argue that under the old system, 34 per cent of initial visa applications were refused on the basis of judgements made by entry clearance officers, but at appeal 25 per cent of these were overturned and visas granted. The CBI broadly welcomes the new arrangements but has concerns that the increased obligations on employers might mean that they are expected to act as immigration officials.

WHERE CAN I FIND OUT MORE?

A number of websites provide advice to candidates, with (for example) automatic skills points calculators for different countries. For the UK Highly Skilled Migrant Programme introduced in January 2002, and for general work permit advice, useful calculators and other information are available at:

http://www.workpermit.com/uk/hsmp_calculator.htm
http://www.globalvisas.com/page21_immigration_and_work_permit_home_page.aspx
http://www.permits2work.co.uk/

Advice on work permit requirements for various skills groups for the UK can be found at:

http://www.skillclear.co.uk/index2.asp

ENDNOTES

1   See for example: System to point way to Australia. *BBC News Webpage*. eMonday, 7 February 2005, 16:17 GMT Migration: How points would work. *BBC News Webpage*. Tuesday, 21 June 2005, 10:10 GMT 11:10 UK

2   There are a number of solicitors' firms specialising in UK immigration law, and many of these provide basic information websites. Much of the following briefing has been taken from http://www.breytenbachs.com

3   McCall, B. (2006) Government agrees to release details of visa regime. *Times Higher Education*, 10 February. 4.

INTERNATIONAL RECRUITMENT FOR EMPLOYMENT IN HOME MARKETS   **4**

❖ **HR professionals face a complex set of issues regarding migrant workers**

❖ **How the NHS is tackling international recruitment (appropriate qualifications, language skills, retention, avoidance of 'poaching' from target countries)**

❖ **The NHS needs active and passive recruitment policies and to remain attractive to talented labour overseas**

❖ **UK organisations may look overseas for recruits prematurely**

What do the developments discussed in the previous chapters mean for the HR professional? The key issues that arise from this international migration of talented labour and the new ways in which it will be regulated are:

❖ establishing where professional expertise and technical insight lies (which sector bodies, HR networks, agencies and service providers can help)

❖ deciding whether the initiative requires a targeted campaign or a longer-term strategic move to sourcing from specific countries or regions

❖ understanding and establishing the base technical competence of recruits and setting up assessment processes where necessary

❖ considering the ethical and reputational issues associated with a campaign

❖ ensuring that there is a local infrastructure in receiving units to handle the increasing workforce diversity that results from successful campaigns

❖ building the reputation of the receiving unit, operation or area so that it can be seen as internationally competitive and attractive (thereby aiding subsequent retention and the success of future campaigns).

The situation in the NHS shows the complex issues faced by many HR professionals in coping with overseas recruitment. Although overall just 4% of nurses nationally (by 2003) had *qualified* overseas (14% of those in London, however), the flow of new and young nurses has become highly internationalised. In 2002/3 43% of new nurse registrants were from abroad. The number of work permits issued to foreign nurses nearly doubled from 2000 to 2003. The vast majority of nurses arriving in London in the last ten years are from just six countries – the Philippines, South Africa,

Australia, New Zealand, Nigeria and Ghana. International recruitment happens at a number of levels.

> 'The vast majority of nurses arriving in London in the last ten years are from just six countries...'

The flow of skilled professionals has also become more internationalised. In each year from 1993 to 2002, nearly half of all new registrants to the General Medical Council were from abroad, increasing to nearly two-thirds by 2003. The peak of international recruitment has probably now passed in this sector, but will form a continuing activity.

We can learn much from the experience of the NHS, as there has been previous research into the experience at Trust level of coping with international recruitment and an analysis of the nature and operation of competitor overseas labour markets.[1] Private sector firms often do not have such detailed intelligence to work from, though the above topics signal the areas they need to explore. What does public sector experience reveal? The case below outlines the issues for South East London NHS Strategic Health Authority (SHA).

THE MANAGEMENT OF THE INTERNATIONAL RESOURCING OF HEALTHCARE PROFESSIONALS[2]

The NHS is the largest single employer within the UK, employing over a million people, 5% of the working population. There are numerous careers in over 70 professions. The NHS has a long history of welcoming staff from overseas to gain experience and education by working in the many different parts of the NHS in England. The NHS is also anxious to reflect the local population it serves. To this end, it actively encourages applicants from a range of backgrounds, regardless of gender, age, religion or race, to apply for jobs. Applications are particularly welcome from professionally qualified healthcare staff from outside the UK.

The Department of Health believes that 'international recruitment has a long-standing and positive place in the NHS. Handled properly and responsibly, international recruitment has benefits for the NHS, individuals and their families. However, international recruitment is an option mainly used by employers trying to fill vacancies in particular geographical areas or medical specialties with recognised shortages.'[3] In practice, an NHS Trust is unlikely to go through the time-consuming and expensive process of international recruitment if a post can be filled within the UK. Work permits are required for applicants from outside the EEA, and NHS employers are not able to get a work permit for an applicant if the post can be filled by a UK or EEA resident. NHS employers may indicate in their advertisements whether applicants from outside the UK will be considered.

Demand, however, has been such that international recruitment has come to play a significant role in resolving resourcing problems. When the NHS Plan 2000 was launched, targets were set to grow the NHS workforce by 2,000 more GPs, 7,500 more consultants, 20,000 more nurses and 6,500 more allied health professionals (AHPs) by March 2004. When new targets were set for 2008, the demand was for 1,500 more consultants and GPs, 35,000 more nurses and midwives, and 30,000 more AHPs. It was recognised that it would not be feasible to recruit all of these additional staff from within the UK. It would also be necessary to focus on retention strategies and new terms and conditions of employment in addition to identifying innovative ways to recruit.

This case study reviews the experience of the NHS in general and the South East London Strategic Health Authority in particular, in dealing with international recruitment. The need for international recruitment in the SHA is inextricably linked to the issue of demand for skills. Since the pioneering work done in the NHS to help resolve skills shortages through international recruitment this demand has evolved. At a practical level this means that HR professionals with time dedicated to managing international recruitment find that the nature of their role changes in line with the level of demand for candidates, but also in line with a set of evolving needs. For example, in the 1960s nurses in the NHS were mainly being recruited into lower-grade posts. More recently the focus has changed, so that the process to attract international candidates has become more of a managed process; attention is also shifting to the challenges that follow, which include retention and career development.

International recruitment in broader context

Given that international recruitment is primarily driven by the need to address demand and associated skills shortages, retention is an important issue. Retention strategies in the NHS are generic to all staff – not just international recruits – and initiatives include Improving Working Lives, which is a blueprint by which NHS employers and staff can measure the management of human resources. The Golden Hello Scheme, which was replaced by the Primary Care Development Scheme in 2005, was designed to promote the retention of GPs. The subsequent Primary Care Development Scheme also includes other primary care staff. The flexible career scheme for doctors facilitates consultants and GPs to work part time, and the new consultant entry scheme, subsequently replaced by the specialist development scheme, enables newly qualified consultants to take their first consultancy post for six months with additional support before committing to a substantive post.

New terms and conditions of employment for NHS employees were introduced, including Agenda for Change. This is a single-job evaluation scheme with a grading structure to cover all jobs in the NHS to support a review of pay and all other terms of employment and the Knowledge and Skills Framework, which is a framework to define the knowledge and skills NHS staff need in order to deliver quality services. New contracts were also negotiated for consultants (the New Consultant Contract) and for GPs (the General Medical Services contract).

Recruitment strategies include financial support for heathcare professionals to return to practice after a career break, increased commissioning of education places for healthcare professionals, and a flexible training scheme for doctors training as consultants and GPs, which enables them to train on a part-time basis. One of the challenges facing HR professionals is the range of skills and jobgroups for which tried and tested schemes exist. In general, more assistance is in place from the Department of Health to help manage international recruitment of doctors, with less support for the recruitment of nurses and associated healthcare professionals.

Different sources of expertise

The Department of Health operates at a *national* level. It has established codes of practice and ethical policies, setting up (for example) government-to-government agreements with some countries to ensure that UK recruitment drives do not strip other national health systems of talent. These agreements exist with India, the Philippines, and Spain. Demand across these countries varies over time. For example, the main source of nurses has shifted in recent years from the Philippines to India.

A number of schemes therefore assisted international recruitment at SHA level but were managed at Department of Health level, such as:

❖ global advertising campaigns: for example, a programme for doctors used web-based recruitment for consultants and GPs, targeted at specific countries. The Department of Health managed the programme and offered a series of careers fairs in the UK.

❖ an International Fellowship Scheme designed to attract specialist consultants in short supply. The targets for this scheme have now been met, and so central funding is no longer necessary.

❖ national web gateways and regional initiatives: for example, the Department of Health had a recent focus on recruiting from Spain.

The Department of Health website makes it clear to potential candidates that competition for junior doctor posts in the UK is very high and is increasing. By the end of 2005 there were on average 493 applicants per junior doctor advertisement – 10 adverts attracted more than 1,000 applicants. Medical graduates are informed that the UK welcomes them 'but would like them to be fully aware of the very high level of competition for junior doctors' posts and the possibility of spending long periods of time unemployed'. Where possible, Trusts seek to recruit from UK candidates. The demand for skills, however, does mean that international candidates will be more likely to be recruited from overseas if they are: consultants in accident and emergency, anaesthesia, child and adolescent psychiatry, old age psychiatry and radiology; dentists; or radiographers. The main attractions – or value proposition – that are communicated on websites include good conditions of employment, teamworking, a culture of lifelong learning and continuous improvement in clinical care, study leave allowance, competitive salaries and generous annual leave.

Codes of Practice

Codes of Practice for the international recruitment can be very important for all organisations, but clearly are critical for the recruitment of healthcare professionals. NHS Jobs adheres to the Code of Practice for the International Recruitment of Healthcare Professionals, in order to promote the best possible standards in international recruitment, and discourage any inappropriate practices that could harm other countries' healthcare systems or the interests of those who apply for posts. There are dozens of agencies that might be used by any particular Trust. In the early days of expansion of services in this area, this was a lucrative business for agencies. This carries both reputational and technical risks for the purchasers of these services if the conduct is not appropriate.

The content of the Code of Practice has evolved over time – it is now on its third iteration – as more has been learned about the management of international recruitment. The Code has moved from offering general guidance to much tighter specification of recruitment practice relating to specific country practice, financial arrangements with applicants and recruitment processes. Trusts are now advised not to use recruitment agencies that have not signed up to the Code. A Department of Health website has a list of agencies that have signed up to the Code, and service providers may be removed.

Experience shows that as demand for skills evolves, the benefits associated with some of the schemes designed to meet short-term skills needs can begin to have a different effect. For example, schemes that were designed to attract consultants on two-year contracts had financial incentives suited to candidates taking a sabbatical from home countries. Encouraging such job groups to continue in employment for a longer term requires a change in the conditions and incentives offered.

A range of options

All NHS recruitment is handled at a local level by individual Trusts, and the type of vacancies and the willingness to recruit from overseas varies greatly across England. There is therefore also an experience base at regional level through SHAs, regional networks of HR professionals and of course within individual Trusts. Professional and institutional bodies such as the Royal Colleges or the King's Fund[4] have expertise in the area, as well as private recruitment agencies.

In addition to using the various Department of Health programmes noted above, South East London SHA therefore uses other options such as:

❖ recruitment agencies: for example, although Trusts do their own assessment, agencies often have good contacts to enable them to carry out overseas interviews.

❖ attracting overseas healthcare professionals living in the UK: the SHA encourages professionals already working here to register their job interest online. In London, for example, there would be hundreds of people who might want to work in the NHS but who need to be facilitated to achieve registration with the relevant professional body and to find appropriate employment. This is not seen therefore as a passive recruitment strategy.

❖ local online information sources: the SHA has a website that provides a lot of information about living and working in south-east London. In considering what information to provide, the SHA sought feedback from successful candidates about what they needed to know.

❖ encouraging refugees with appropriate experience to apply for jobs: there are, for example, refugees who have healthcare qualifications that are not recognised, but the Skills Escalator programme in the NHS means that they may now be able to see where their skills are relevant.

❖ using exchange schemes: Trusts provide clinical placements for nurses from developing countries to enable them to develop their skills and to study for a master's degree. These clinicians then return to their country of origin with new and updated skills and knowledge.

Selection and assessment procedures

The selection and assessment procedures are different for each professional group. Overseas healthcare professionals are required to meet the registration requirements of the relevant professional bodies, of which there are four:

❖ doctors – General Medical Council (GMC)

❖ dentists – General Dental Council (GDC)

❖ nurses and midwives – Nursing & Midwifery Council (NMC)

❖ allied health professionals – Health Professions Council (HPC).

For example, for non-EU junior doctors there is a General Medical Council Professional and Linguistic Assessment Board. For consultants and GPs procedures include assessment of clinical competence, language assessment and an interview panel in the UK. Good practice is for the candidate's partner and family to be invited to attend when the doctor attends for interview. They are provided with an introduction to the organisation and its locality, and they meet prospective peers.

For dentists, the GDC International qualifying exam has three parts (for non-EU candidates), and there is an assessment of clinical competence, language assessment and an interview panel run in their own country. For nurses and allied health professionals there is usually a written assessment of clinical knowledge, language assessment and an interview in their own country, and use is made of videoconferencing and telephone interviews.

When using telephone or video interviews, the checks necessary to verify that the person being interviewed is the candidate have to be carried out by local agencies or government visa departments. Non-EU nurses and midwives and EU AHPs also undertake a period of supervised practice in the UK, prior to registration, of 3 to 12 months.

Across all of these occupational groups, the assessment of English language competence is a crucial issue. Two basic aspects of English language competence need to be established:

❖ levels of language proficiency that ensure safe and skilled communication with all stakeholders

❖ levels of knowledge and effectiveness comparable with UK vocational and educational standards.

In the NHS there are national proficiency tests relevant for professional clinical competency and English language capability. Non-EU overseas healthcare professionals are required to demonstrate English language competence (International English Language Testing System) to the relevant professional body prior to registration:

❖ GMC – IELTS 7.0

❖ GDC – IELTS 7.0

❖ NMC – IELTS 6.5

❖ HPC – IELTS 7.0, or comparable qualification.

Depending on the locality, other service providers may be used. For example, when recruiting in Spain, the British Council were able to offer their language assessors to the Department of Health to carry out local language assessments.

Prior to arrival, a range of other issues have to be managed. These include occupational health clearance, Criminal Records Bureau clearance, references, registration with the professional body, work permit applications and assistance with finding accommodation and schools for children.

Induction process

The induction process is very important. At South East London SHA induction includes an orientation to the employing organisation and the NHS, the multi-disciplinary team, colloquial English and accents, the multi-cultural population in the locality, policies and procedures, and new ways of working, for instance on-call arrangements. All NHS employers are encouraged to arrange an induction programme which covers: a welcome and introduction to life in England; discussion of cultural factors which candidates will need to know and understand; induction into the clinical aspects of the job; and other relevant medical issues, including legal aspects of medical practice in England. Employers, in consultation with the candidate, appoint a colleague to act as a professional mentor to discuss continuing professional development and the opportunities for study. A member of staff is identified to ensure pastoral support and advice during the transition to working in the NHS and settling into life in England. This may include introduction to social and professional networks for doctors and their families. Clearly, this activity serves as a retention role as well and is part of a general focus on providing ongoing support in terms of access to education and training, improving working lives, partner employment and childcare.

Key lessons learned

What have been the main lessons learned? The success of international recruitment activity in the SHA is judged in terms of the ability to meet performance targets, the delivery of care, and the ability to integrate international candidates into the workforce. A number of lessons have been learned about international recruitment:

❖ It is essential to gain support of professional bodies. International recruitment programmes can be lengthy in duration and support of these bodies can help speed this up by overcoming potential obstacles.

❖ It is also important to get sign-up from clinicians. There are a number of ongoing issues that have to be managed by HR professionals (ranging from the existence of other people who can provide additional support and mentoring, on the positive side, through to discrimination, on the negative). The receiving units for overseas workers need to be actively engaged with the whole range of issues that might be faced across the employment relationship.

❖ Everyone in the organisation should be informed of the plan to recruit from overseas so that the need for the strategy and the importance of its success is understood.

❖ Cultural differences can be overcome, but are unavoidable. Many of these differences are understood early, but other subtle effects are seen over time. For example, as more insight is gained into the different nature of professional competencies and skills, then the need for shadowing or mentorship may become more apparent.

❖ HR professionals have to ensure that overseas candidates are treated fairly throughout their tenure with the organisation, but there might be cultural reasons why, for example, one group might not be strongly represented across career grades. For example, tacit learning has suggested that in comparison with nurses from India, nurses from the Philippines may be less likely to apply voluntarily for promotion or further training. Attention has to be given to mentoring to encourage movement and ensure that those with potential consider advancement. Indirectly, the impact of attitudes to career-advancement has been the development of

a bottleneck in entry-level roles.

❖ Recruiting units must be able to demonstrate clinical competence of international recruits to staff and patients.

❖ Candidates and employers should not underestimate how hard it is to learn English to a competent level. IELTS grades do not ensure good communication. For the NHS it is the quality of communication that is essential. The technical assessment of linguistic capability often has to be supplemented by mandatory communication courses. EU candidates do not have to have the IELTS requirement, so where Trusts insist on communication courses, this can create candidate issues that have to be managed.

❖ If the family is not committed to move to the UK, then retention becomes an issue. The situation is identical to that of recruiting expatriates – partner and family issues are very important.

❖ It is not always necessary to go overseas.

As the South East London SHA case shows, HR professionals need to understand the often complex web of best practice and expertise that exists in such situations. The experience of the NHS shows that any firms attempting to source employees internationally need three kinds of strategy:

❖ active recruitment policies: where specific skillgroups and countries are targeted, arrangements with service providers need to be established, different media and channels to the labour market known and tested, overseas recruitment trips normalised and codes of practice reflected in internal practice.

❖ passive recruitment policies: where the applicants take the initiative and organisations need to be able to capitalise on this, or where organisations may capture employees simply because there has been an increase in both the 'flow' and 'stock' of international employees or qualified refugees. These include provision of one-stop access to personal career advice for interested employees, with details of professional regulations and immigration requirements, and relationship development (on-location visibility, internship arrangement and so forth) with significant sources of international employees such as universities.

❖ longer-term strategies to ensure the continued ability to compete in international labour markets. A wide range of countries are similarly demanding international employees. The UK, and London, has become a market for the forward-brokerage of many skilled employees to other English-speaking countries, and organisations need to develop strategies to ensure that they (and their location) can attract talented employees.

INTERNATIONAL RECRUITMENT FOR EMPLOYMENT IN HOME MARKETS

Experience in the NHS in general also shows that the need for international recruitment can be cyclical. Demand pressures – and subsequent skills shortages – are a critical factor. There are ways other than international recruitment that can help manage this demand. In some organisations the need for international recruitment may be lessened by contracting work to other suppliers. For the NHS, the impact of this on the international recruitment process has *not* been very significant – the programmes outlined in the case above have had a more direct effect – but the process is mentioned by way of illustrating *potential* links between overall resourcing policies and demand for staff within any particular area.

> **'Overseas clinical teams are a flexible resource to help the NHS offer choice...'**

The goal of the NHS is to 'ensure that patients and service users have rapid access to personalised health and social care services that they need and choose; and that those services are delivered by a world-class workforce with the capacity to achieve this objective'. The approach involved a range of policies. For example, as part of the drive to treat more patients and reduce waiting times, the NHS has started referring certain patients to other parts of the European Economic Area (EEA) for treatment, and since July 2002 a number of projects using overseas clinical teams have been in place in England, providing extra capacity locally. These cover a range of specialities, such as general surgery, orthopaedics and ophthalmology, and have treated over 10,000 patients in 17 schemes. Overseas clinical teams are a flexible resource to help the NHS offer choice and to manage their waiting list demand. Using overseas teams differs from traditional recruitment because in most cases it is based on relatively short periods of activity or the use of rotating teams (for example, several sessions over a few days or a rotation over the course of a few weeks) rather than full-time working, because the clinical staff concerned continue to practise overseas. The decision to use an overseas clinical team is made locally, following consultation with local staff.

> **'...the very success of the original international recruitment campaigns for overseas doctors...has led to an entry-level and promotion blockage for UK candidates...'**

A key message from recent developments is that employers need to understand the long-term reputational implications of plugging short-term skills gaps through reliance on international recruitment. For example, as a consequence of an increase in the supply of UK graduates from medical schools and government changes to immigration policy that require preference be given to EU doctors, five years after the launch of a range of international recruitment policies and practices demand for overseas doctors from outside the EU has fallen dramatically. Two internal pressures are likely to reduce demand. Recruiting bodies now have to report on how many international applicants there were, how many were short-listed and why an EU national was not preferable. The fear is that recruiters may find a threshold-competent applicant from within the EU, so this person would be fast-tracked in preference

to a more highly qualified non-EU doctor. Moreover, the very success of the original international recruitment campaigns for overseas doctors (the number of overseas doctors sitting the BMC's entrance exam has trebled from 2,000 to over 6,000) has led to an entry-level and promotion blockage for UK candidates (the number of medical graduates from UK universities has grown now to levels higher than ever before).

The experiences of the public sector seeking out talented employees from overseas labour markets outlined above are likely to spread into many private business sectors. For example, the Smiths Group (which operates in aerospace and medical sectors) has 38,000 employees spread across four global divisions. It developed a corporate extranet (based on the Internet but only accessible to internal employees) that could be used to search for jobs by career path, location and division.[5] They saw this development as being the first of many that will come about as the recruitment industry becomes increasingly globalised. Similarly, Shell has overcome one of its barriers to mobility – staff putting themselves forward for overseas postings – by switching away from central planning to an open resourcing system in which jobs designated as overseas appointments are posted for anyone to apply to rather than first selecting individuals and then persuading them to relocate.[6]

There is a risk, however, that firms may be tempted to use the Internet for overseas recruitment as part of their solution to skills shortages. Technology has both advantages and disadvantages, and there has been some debate about the temptation for firms facing skills shortages in the UK to jump too quickly to e-enabled recruitment in overseas labour markets. So how should an organisation judge the success of international recruitment campaigns? In addition to issues of competence, the success (or not) is generally *not* assessed in terms of the cost-effectiveness of salary levels. Rather, it is measured in terms of:

❖ subsequent retention levels and reduction in vacancy levels

❖ effective integration of internationally recruited staff into the systems and culture of the organisation

❖ minimal additional time needed to ensure individual support and development and integration into effective teams.

The latter issue cannot be avoided, and therefore, although beyond the scope of this report, international employees need to be protected by UK employment law in the same way as domestic employees, and policies and practice need to ensure that access to training and career development is equally afforded. Many employers do not yet record their employment of international employees, making the assessment of their needs and effectiveness more problematic.

ENDNOTES

1   My thanks to Dr Ruth Young and her work in this area. See for example: King's Fund (2004) *London calling: the international recruitment of health workers to the capital.* London: King's Fund Publications; National Primary Care Research and Development Centre (2003) The international market for medical doctors: perspectives on the positioning of the UK. *Executive Summary No. 28.* University of Manchester: Manchester Centre for Healthcare Management.

2   This case study is by Sarah Coleby, Assistant Director of Workforce
    Development, South East London Strategic Health Authority. It is
    based on an analysis presented at a CIPD Forum in 2005 and updated
    in February 2006. Additional background research material has also
    been gathered from the Department of Health and SELWDC websites
    www.selwdc.nhs.uk and other research into the NHS.

3   Department of Health website http://www.dh.gov.uk/international
    accessed on 13 February 2006.

4   King's Fund (2004) *London calling: the international recruitment of
    health workers to the capital.* London: King's Fund Publications.

5   Ford, H. (2002) World of difference. *People Management.* 27 June.
    38–40.

6   Johnson, R. (2003) Final destination. *People Management.* Vol. 9, No.
    2. 40–43.

RESOURCING SPECIALIST SKILLS FOR USE IN HOME AND OVERSEAS MARKETS

5

❖ **The BBC World Service relies on its brand for recruitment**

❖ **Overseas (local) centres are used to assess shortlisted candidates**

❖ **The World Service Trust has the demanding task of making programmes driven by local issues but managed from London**

The NHS case study in Chapter 4 reflects the issues involved in having to conduct recruitment campaigns in overseas and home markets in order to address home-country skills shortages. For other organisations, the ability to be able to resource professionals and specialist skills in an overseas labour market is part and parcel of their operations. The second case study below provides insight into the practical issues involved in this latter context. It examines international recruitment at the BBC World Service.

INTERNATIONAL RECRUITMENT IN THE BBC WORLD SERVICE[1]

Within the BBC, international recruitment activity moved from World Service Broadcasting to BBC People in April 2004. The BBC World Service broadcasts in 43 languages, including (of course) English, to 148 million people across the world. It is a small arm of the BBC that is funded by the British Foreign Office to bring benefit to Britain, but it must also be editorially impartial and independent in its broadcasting. Recruitment can be in the UK or in the local countries. It competes for audience figures with different organisations, depending on the geography, such as Voice of America, Radio Monte Carlo, Al Jazeera (in the Middle East) and Radio Free Europe (in Eastern Europe and the former Soviet Union). The World Service also operates differently around the world. Partnerships may be formed with local radio channels to broadcast the BBC news on FM. Approximately 500 people are employed worldwide in the Division.

The World Service knows that in terms of audience figures, the timing of broadcasts and the use of FM relay (FM reception is better than shortwave) are important factors, but in terms of competing both for listeners and

for job applicants around the world, the most important factor is the BBC brand. The BBC aims to be the best radio and television broadcaster in the world, broadcasting in an independent, impartial and informative way. When recruiting, it wants to give people opportunities that they may not get from their current employers, for example to develop their skills and work in an international market.

To support this brand, work was done centrally and formally to develop six corporate values:

1 Trust is the foundation of the BBC: we are independent, impartial and honest.

2 Audiences are at the heart of everything we do.

3 We take pride in developing quality and value for money.

4 Creativity is the lifeblood of the organisation.

5 We respect each other and celebrate our diversity.

6 We are one BBC; great things happen when we work together.

These were translated into policies, one of which covered recruitment. The BBC develops a clear brand in its recruitment, a fact that the brochures for the BBC World Service reflect with the following adjectives: international; trustworthy; award-winning; accessible; impartial; educational; and online.

The BBC World Service also includes around 550 staff in BBC Monitoring who are based primarily in Caversham,

Berkshire but who also have a presence in a number of overseas offices. The purpose of BBC Monitoring is to collate information about the reporting of news stories in the different media around the world. Monitoring is funded by a number of stakeholders such as the Cabinet Office who have use for this material.

The nature of international recruitment activity

The international recruitment team comprises a recruitment account manager, three recruitment consultants and six recruitment advisers. The recruitment account manager manages the team, which as a whole provides expertise in international recruitment. In addition, the recruitment account manager manages a small team at BBC World Service Monitoring, which comprises a recruitment consultant and associate recruitment consultant.

The bulk of international recruitment activity is concerned with two activities:

❖ recruiting journalists (producers) for the language services of the World Service. The number of staff working in specific-language services ranges from 3 to 120. These producers are offered employment contracts under English law, normally on a continuing (pensionable) basis.

❖ recruiting staff to work in the World Service Trust overseas They work on particular projects for limited periods of time. This is outlined later in the case study.

Recruiting internationally for World Service language services

For the first area of recruitment, the manager and consultants work on campaigns in particular areas of the world, running the campaigns, offering advice and expertise, making applications for work permits and assisting new recruits with visa applications. In addition, they interview for some posts, making job offers to successful candidates, and provide training for new managers. Recruitment advisers report to the recruitment manager/consultants and carry out the administration work, including setting up assessments in the UK and overseas and record-keeping for recruitment campaigns.

The policy is for the BBC to trawl the UK first for candidates and then in the target countries and the surrounding region. Recruiting internationally relies on organising every aspect of a recruitment campaign across different countries at the same time. This makes the jobs more complex than for staff who recruit within the UK. With years of experience within the World Service, they have developed expertise and knowledge of the business and an understanding of how to fit diverse individuals into the organisation.

An international recruitment campaign might consist of advertising in and receiving applications from many countries within one region and worldwide (for example, a recent Arabic campaign received applications from 34 countries). The recruitment team then arrange for selection assessments (written journalistic and language skills and voice tests) to be held across these countries at a similar time, sending out test materials, arranging for candidates and invigilators to be present and also for the return of completed test materials.

The team then arrange for blind marking of the tests to prevent any bias and collate the results, subsequently setting up interviews in different countries. On completion, they then send out offer packs, apply for work permits and visas, arrange flights and initial accommodation in the BBC's residential accommodation, Beaumont House, for new recruits (and their families if applicable) when they first arrive in London. In addition, they organise their induction timetables and training course placements, assist them with opening bank accounts in the UK and applying for National Insurance Numbers. The team also keep records of the expiry dates of staff's work permits and leave to remain in the UK and apply for extensions to these if required. In addition, the World Service Recruitment team works closely with staff at Beaumont House and a relocations support co-ordinator who provides advice and support to help new recruits from overseas to settle into life in the UK, including finding accommodation, schools and so on.

When running a recruitment campaign in an overseas country, the World Service Recruitment team advertises in the newspapers that they expect journalists to read and, increasingly, uses the BBC website. Decisions on where to place job advertisements rely on the judgement and experience of the manager and consultants and the recruiting managers within the specific language service, who are able to advise about the publications that other journalists would be likely to read in a particular country. The value of advertising in particular publications is weighed against the cost and the number of applications generated by each publication from previous recruitment campaigns.

Experience has shown that, in some countries, a single job advertisement is likely to generate thousands of responses, regardless of whether applicants have the specified skills and experience. All of these have to be reviewed and shortlisted or rejected (in writing). In such circumstances, more use is made of the local network – for example, by placing a notice in the Journalists' Club.

The World Service looks first and foremost for journalists who can work in radio and online. They are sometimes recruited from broadcasting organisations but can also come from a newspaper or online background.

Recruitment campaigns are co-ordinated with centres overseas that conduct/invigilate assessments for shortlisted candidates on their behalf. These assessments are designed to assess a number of competencies for producers and are provided by the head of the individual language services – the main area is translation from English to the vernacular language in a journalistic context, but candidates are also judged on editorial content, running order and the treatment of stories on radio and online. They must also have a voice test for radio suitability.

The producers need to have the local language as their first or best language, but they must also have an excellent comprehension of English because their main sources are the BBC Newsroom in London. The priority and running order of news items may differ according to the audience but, as BBC output, it is essential that they be translated accurately and impartially. However, as in other service organisations that recruit internationally, such as the NHS, there is a need to possess a higher contextual understanding of a language as well as being proficient, because there are potentially high risks involved if misunderstandings occur. In the NHS, communication between a doctor and a foreign-born nurse, for example, must be clear. Although BBC World Service is recruiting foreign nationals, the level of English proficiency is crucially important, given the risks of poor or misunderstood communication.

Once recruited, appointees attend four weeks of training, the first two being a journalism course taught in English, which also means they need to be able to focus and express themselves fully in English. Prior to this, on arrival, they undergo an English language assessment and then are offered English language lessons on a one-to-one basis with the BBC's English Language Development team.

In the last few years, the manager and recruitment consultants have also been asked by managers for advice on entry requirements, appropriate contracts and remuneration for visiting professionals from bureaus abroad and for other BBC employees working on placements overseas. When a large operation is being set up abroad, it is the responsibility of the project/business manager involved to find out about local employment, tax and national insurance legislation, and visa and entry requirements. As new offices are established throughout the world, lawyers are employed to ensure that staff conditions and rates of pay are compatible with those in the local labour market. In some areas, such as Poland and the Czech Republic, for example, the local offices are of sufficient scale to be able to handle local recruitment initiatives.

Methods of assessing candidates

London-based producers in the World Service work within their own culture in terms of the language they use, the people with whom they work and the audiences in their target area. They need to have up-to-date knowledge about their target area but they broadcast under BBC values. Candidates are tested on their technical skills, their language skills, the suitability of their voice for radio and the ability to write and work for radio and online. They also need to be creative and come up with programme ideas that are of interest to and engage with the people in their markets.

The recruitment assessment for producers was developed originally as a template by BBC Assessment and Development and has been adapted by the Language Services of the BBC World Service for each individual service. It is very much a sample of the work that a producer would be required to do in each Service. Skills assessed include translation, writing for radio and online, knowledge of target area and international affairs, and editorial judgement.

The BBC is trying to develop ways to assess people's 'softer' skills which are not always shown in a written assessment – diplomacy, leadership, strategic thinking, planning and organising skills, and the ability to keep their team happy. Candidates for some positions also complete an Occupational Personality Questionnaire (OPQ) and/or a role-play that assesses various aspects of the job, including communication. The OPQ used shows leadership preferences, and these are discussed further in the interview, as people may need to work in a different way from their preferred way of doing something. The OPQ is carried out by one of the BBC's internal Recruitment Consultants.

The OPQ was piloted and then made obligatory in the recruitment of senior managers. It has only recently been used in the recruitment process for language service managers at the BBC World Service. There is an awareness of the need to ensure that judgements are moderated because of possible biases that might be explained by the cross-cultural validity of the test. Many overseas applicants could achieve lower consistency and lower scores (see Chapter 13 on cross-cultural testing), and therefore it is important to investigate a candidate's language skills further in an interview. For example, in the recruitment of producers, there have been instances where a person's translation was technically perfect but their speaking and fluency in English was not as strong, so they could not be easily understood at interview. Communicating and interacting with colleagues are essential abilities for a good producer.

Role-plays have been developed over the last few years by a team of occupational psychologists based in BBC People (Assessment and Development) to ensure that the recruitment of managers within the BBC was not based solely on interviews.

Recruiting internationally for the World Service Trust

The World Service Trust is an independent charity set up in 1999 that works within the BBC World Service and aims to reduce poverty through the innovative use of the media in developing countries and countries in transition and to help build media expertise within those countries.

In the last three years, the World Service Trust has grown significantly, funding increasing from £3 million to £13.5 million. It works both on small- and large-scale projects. It needs to recruit very specialised skills – for example, people with media skills, but also people with experience of global issues that might be being featured, such as HIV/AIDS, dysentery and so forth.

Recruiting project managers and programme-makers internationally

The people working for the Trust make media programmes for developing countries. Their role is demanding, because they must ensure that they have an independent and impartial approach, while making programmes that effect behaviour change. Where possible, people are recruited locally, but the skills required may not be available in the labour market in some developing countries.

In many international organisations, one of the challenges is to understand what the local issues are and adapt provision accordingly. The World Service Trust also has the challenge of managing projects that are driven by local conditions but are managed from London. Projects – whether, for example, the use of condoms in the fight against AIDS, the use of mosquito nets and drinking water in campaigns to raise awareness about the transmission of diseases, etc – must be relevant locally and must try to effect behaviour change. Although the ultimate aim is to run projects locally, the requirements to report to the Trust's governors in London and to ensure that programmes are in line with the BBC's image demand exceptional managerial expertise.

Programmes are made for particular countries and cultures. For example, India has a popular, award-winning soap series which is a drama about HIV/AIDS. In Africa, the radio stations are usually local and reach a wide audience. They may require a travelling group to engage people. The aim then is to reach as many people as possible by using the media available, including the Internet if available, and then adapting ways of doing things to the local situation.

The complexity of having customers, for whom programmes are made, in local markets while having UK-based sponsors and meeting the demands of making programmes which fit into the BBC's ethos make it challenging to recruit the right people.

Balancing candidate performance with other issues

There is, however, a potential risk in being driven too much by concerns of English proficiency and test performance when the key competence in the World Service is proficiency in vernacular languages and cultural/political knowledge of the country to which they are broadcasting. International recruiters also have to balance other judgements. When recruiting foreign nationals, there is a risk that test performance begins to favour candidates from specific countries, which could lead to claims of unlawful discrimination. In a setting such as the BBC World Service, where the diversity of the candidate base and perceived fairness are also issues, attention has to be given to the overall profile of candidates.

Judging the success of an international recruitment campaign

This then raises another important issue for international recruiters. How can the success of a campaign be judged? The BBC World Service does have an eight-month probationary review period for all staff recruited on continuing (pensionable) contracts, and all staff have annual performance appraisals. Managers should regularly monitor the performance of staff, including their effectiveness, and they will also look at how well they have integrated into the organisation. The progress made in Services in particular regions is discussed at managers' and senior managers' meetings. If targets for website hits and listener numbers are not met, managers try to analyse whether this is because of the mix of expertise within their team or because of the success of competitor initiatives. This may have an impact on future recruitment campaigns if it highlights a missing element in the team.

ENDNOTE

1   This case is based on interviews with Jenny Dunbar, Recruitment Consultant, BBC World Service.

SHARED SERVICES AND GLOBAL RECRUITMENT

6

❖ **Recruitment policy is affected by general moves towards shared-service structures and e-technology**

❖ **The use of technical platforms for delivering HR varies according to business sector**

The agenda for those involved in international recruitment, selection and assessment is often determined by the current drive towards the use of technology and the attractions of a shared-service model in this area. For BBC People, for example, judgements about how best to organise international recruitment activity are bound up in general changes in HR delivery that have been taking place over the last three years. As part of its general restructuring, the BBC has undergone two waves of downsizing. The elimination of 3,780 jobs amounted to 19% of its UK workforce, or nearly 14% of its worldwide staff of 27,000.[1] HR was centralised and a business-partner model was introduced in the divisions. As part of the process, a number of professional services, including parts of HR, are being outsourced. BBC People will be reduced from around 1,000 staff to 450 as part of a three-year change programme[2] and a 10-year outsourcing deal worth £100 million and saving £50 million. This involves a partial outsourcing process, in which about 260 jobs moved to Capita (in Belfast) on 1 April 2006, transfer of posts to elsewhere in the BBC and the loss of 180 jobs.

> 'For BBC People...judgements about how best to organise international recruitment activity are bound up in general changes in HR delivery...'

A list of 11 areas for possible outsourcing was drawn up around resourcing, remuneration, contracting, relocation, disability access services, HR advice and occupational health, and the conduct of international recruitment comes under this remit.[3] The functions finally outsourced include recruitment, pay and benefits (excluding pensions), assessment, outplacement and some training, HR administration, relocation, occupational health and disability access services. Within the BBC, this means that functions such as HR have to be aligned with strategic objectives, which are to become more creative and audience-focused.

Service delivery will be split from strategic HR (led by a series of heads of HR and Development in each of the 17 divisions). The focus of these roles will be on building capability within divisions. A separate function will focus on service delivery to line managers, driven by service-level agreements. The HR director said:

> I subscribe to the view that we will increasingly have quality organisations that can take some of our services and go one better than we can, because they have developed deep expertise in those services in a way most large organisations cannot.[4]

These changes, then, are part of the general shift towards shared-service structures within HR and the use of technology to enable more self-service delivery, which has led to a separation of transactional services, business partner roles and technical advice functions. The decision that has to be made by all organisations in the context of outsourcing services is whether the technical knowledge inside specialised functions can be protected or whether sufficient expertise is available from an agency. Different solutions may be pursued in relation to the outsourcing or insourcing of international recruitment. Advances in technology and e-enablement of recruitment processes have broadened the scope of geographical intake and introduced new efficiencies, which in some instances means that firms are expanding the scope of their internal recruitment activities.

> 'Advances in technology...have broadened the scope of geographical intake and introduced new efficiencies...'

For example, Nike is to move its recruitment in-house in Europe, the Middle East and Africa to reduce costs and improve the overall quality of the applicants it hires.[5] This decision followed the successful implementation of a software system at Nike's EMEA headquarters in the Netherlands. The system was introduced in 2002 to automate the recruitment process. It enabled applicants to apply directly for both specific jobs and on a speculative basis via Nike's website. Details are retained on file to create a database of future interest that can be searched for specific competencies. Some 8,500 people are currently listed. Applicants are automatically asked to update their CVs every six months for their file to remain active.

From June 2003 to May 2004, a total of 556 positions were filled using the new system, 144 of which came from the future interest database. Nike saved 54% in recruitment costs in the first three years of operation, and reports less reliance on external recruitment and search agencies as a result of the future interest database. The average time to fill vacancies fell from 62 to 42 days, and the cost per hire also diminished. Having already established their own databases, they are now doing their own research for senior-level headhunting and intend to establish an in-house agency for senior recruitment. This move is intended to allow the organisation's resourcing group to play a more consultative and advisory role.

The sector that an organisation operates in has a significant impact on the attractiveness of pursuing common technical platforms for the delivery of HR services. For example, in the banking sector the employee cost-base is variable across organisations and operations, but would be seen as low in comparison with other sectors – typically from 40% to 60%. Given a lower employee cost-base, the pressure to reduce the costs of HR service delivery is not so great as might be seen in other sectors. However, because the banking business model is itself technology-driven, there is an expectation that HR functions should also be run off common technical platforms.

ENDNOTES

1   International Herald Tribune (2005) BBC announces 2050 more job cuts. *International Herald Tribune.* 22 March. 14.

2   Griffiths, J. (2005) BBC gets creative as HR jobs are cut. *People Management.* Vol. 11, No.9. 9.

3   People Management (2005) Three firms in running for BBC outsourcing contracts. *People Management.* Vol. 11, No. 24. 9.

4   Pickard, J. (2006) Conflicting schedule. *People Management.* Vol. 12, No. 5. 14-15.

5   People Management (2005) Nike feels benefit of in-house hiring, *People Management.* Vol. 11, No. 3. 11.

RECRUITMENT IN THE CONTEXT OF AN INTERNATIONALISATION STRATEGY

7

❖ **Barclaycard International is expanding worldwide, while UK staff numbers are going down**

❖ **The HR challenge for Barclaycard is to create HR processes that align with generic policy but are sensitive to local conditions**

❖ **Key to expansion has been the creation of an international resourcing business partner**

Although this report concentrates on international resourcing issues, these cannot be understood without also explaining developments in:

1   expatriate management

2   the process of creating new in-country operations

3   the challenges of managing more strategic aspects of international resourcing during a period of rapid expansion, such as talent management

4   the varied, dynamic and complex nature of the HR business partner role.

> '...it is easy to lose the sense of dynamism, pace and excitement which surrounds an internationalisation strategy.'

As can be seen in the Barclaycard International case study (below), firms can use the development of a multicultural workforce to the advantage of an internationalisation strategy. The case study outlines their experiences and shows how the above HR issues have to be managed as the internationalisation process proceeds. Looking across the case study, and the historical sequence of HR issues that have been managed during the internationalisation process, it is clear then that as a firm globalises, a clear sequence of decisions has to be made as to which HR processes will be managed at a global level and which co-ordinated in-country. The role of local business partners in relation to recruitment and selection activity develops, and the insights into what the central package of HR policies manages to create in behavioural terms in the various local cultures also becomes more sophisticated. In sharing some of the detail behind recent events and placing them into a structured account, it is easy to lose the

sense of dynamism, pace and excitement which surrounds an internationalisation strategy.

BARCLAYCARD INTERNATIONAL: SEEDING EXPANSION[1]

Barclaycard was established in 1966 as part of Barclays Bank PLC. Barclays Bank PLC's strategy has four medium-term themes: to defend and extend UK banking, build new international markets, grow world-class, global-product businesses; and develop operational excellence. One of the ways in which global-product businesses will grow is through the expansion of the cards and loans business. Barclaycard was the UK's first credit card and is now one of the largest global credit card businesses. It has 11.2 million retail customers in the UK, with 3.7 million cards issued internationally (up from 1.28 million cards in 2002 and 1.42 million in 2003). Barclaycard is a multi-brand credit card and consumer-lending business. It is currently one of the leading credit card companies in Europe and is increasing its international presence. Barclaycard encompasses: the Cards & Loans business mostly traded as Barclayloan, FirstPlus, Clydesdale Financial Services and Monument credit cards. Outside the UK, Barclaycard International operates in the USA, Germany, Spain, Greece, Italy, Portugal, Ireland, Sweden, Norway, France, Asia-Pacific and across Africa. Barclaycard International is evolving from a domestic base and has some interesting challenges ahead in doing so.

Barclaycard International first became profitable in 2003, with profits of £4 million. After an alliance with the Standard Bank of South Africa in 2003 and launches the next year in Ireland and Portugal, by 2004 profits had increased to £8 million, despite the investment costs of the international expansion and acquisition. The acquisition of the US credit card issuer Juniper Financial Corporation was completed on 1 December 2004. Acquiring Juniper (rebranded as Barclays USA) was part of Barclaycard International's strategy to become by 2013 as meaningful a contributor to the Group as Barclaycard UK currently is. In order to do this, Barclays will invest significantly in Barclaycard International.

Growth strategy

Barclaycard International has a challenging and rapid growth strategy. If it is to be as successful as its stated ambition, the need for a truly global approach to doing business will become ever more apparent. It employs around 3,000 staff across its portfolio of businesses, of which just 15% are based in the UK. As new international operations are created either as a consequence of joint ventures (JV), acquisitions or through organic growth, this number will continue to increase while the relative percentage of staff based in the UK will diminish. The rapid growth of this business brings its own challenges for the HR function.

The HR director and HR business partners (HRBPs) support the board directors of Barclaycard International and ensure that an end-to-end HR service is provided to employees in every location. For the HRBP the challenge varies in each country but always includes the question of how to ensure rigour and consistency across operations in very different cultures, business markets and labour markets.

One area of focus for the HR director of Barclaycard International is to put a platform of people management processes in place that bring sufficient stability, governance and control, ensure flexibility in global and local decisions, and use this platform to enable rapid future expansion. This means turning what has historically been a UK-centric operation into one guided by a global mindset. The broader agenda requires the establishment of processes, structures and frameworks that provide generic guidance and clarity for country operations but that have sufficient flexibility to accommodate cultural, legal and social factors.

In order to achieve this, the primary agenda items for the HR team in 2006 include international resourcing, international mobility, talent acquisition and development, and global policies and frameworks.

International resourcing
A global approach

One of the key challenges facing Barclaycard International is how to resource and then transfer capability globally, either within an existing business or during start-up and subsequent building of a local business.

To enable Barclaycard to recruit globally, a range of preferred recruitment suppliers are used, from large global recruitment agencies to specialised local firms. Given the nature of country operations, historically relationships with these agencies and suppliers have largely been handled by local HRBPs. The HR community is building up its networks across these agencies and ensuring that it learns how best to manage the different types of agency and understand the true global capability of suppliers as well as the availability of skills in each labour market.

To support the movement of internal employees, HRBPs now make sure that all employees are aware of job opportunities in other countries. There is a common site to share every vacancy between Hamburg, Zaragoza and Dublin, and a frequent exchange of information between country HRBPs. It is proving successful in sourcing applicants and will be extended to all locations in due course.

Recruitment of international resourcing manager

Another consequence of rapid international expansion has been the need to create a dedicated International resourcing business partner. The new role has to act as a support mechanism for HRBPs and business leaders in the acquisition of top talent from the market. There will always be a significant proportion of recruitment activity that is nationally focused. This requires decisions about which resourcing activities need strategic and central oversight, and which can be left to the country-based HRBPs. On the recruitment of the international resourcing manager, they will look to:

❖ negotiate global preferred-supplier arrangements for use of headhunters and research institutions

❖ develop the employee value proposition and employment brand across countries

❖ advise on which processes must be run globally and which should best operate under local contexts

❖ provide a challenge to all sites by signalling sources of best practice

❖ ensure appropriate geographical acquisition and use of international talent.

Central operation

Barclaycard's call centre in Ireland builds the central platform to enable the business to expand. It now employs 360 people, up from a base of only 10 people working in-country in 1997. During this time there has been a remarkable change in terms of international recruitment. Barclaycard's initial intention was to use

Ireland to support non-UK operations. Eight countries are now served out of the Dublin centre, including Ireland, Italy, Spain, France, Germany, Portugal, Greece and Botswana. Dublin was chosen as an early location because of the nature of the role, the employee base and the City's labour market. As a population there is an intention to stay in the country for around 12 to 18 months. They will speak (and are hired for) their mother tongue in the job and markets they serve, but the social interactions in work help improve their English language. The real challenge is the 12–18 month timeframe, as this has driven high levels of attrition.

Spain is an operation that has recently been moved in-country. Eighteen months ago it was served by the Dublin centre, but on the Group acquisition of Banco Zaragozano Barclaycard International took over responsibility for the credit card activity and launched a new contact centre in the country. Because Dublin acted as the central operation, Barclaycard offered employees the chance to move from Dublin to Spain. Around 35 staff moved from Ireland back to Spain.

International mobility
Mobility contract

In order to enable global movement within Barclaycard International, the HR team has devised an international mobility framework. Rapid global expansion requires the business to be able to deploy skills and experience in a multitude of countries at short notice. This cannot always be achieved at pace through local recruitment, so expatriation of current employees is often the best solution. However, employee mobility and the increasing cost and complexity of expatriating individuals need to be considered. The recently devised framework seeks to secure talented employees onto global contracts for which they are paid a premium to be globally mobile. Some 'light' expatriation benefits have been added as a core component of this framework. The concept is now being tested in Barclaycard International.

Process of expatriation and repatriation

There are a number of expatriates on international secondments (these may be drawn from either Barclaycard or the broader Barclays Group). These individuals provide functional expertise and leadership skills to the various countries. Barclaycard International typically uses expatriates either to work with potential business in new countries to support the growth strategy or to provide specialist expertise to other parts of the Barclaycard operations internationally.

The HRBP is key to the set-up of any assignment. The HRBP will work with the business to build up a robust business case, help identify employees, and work with the line manager and individual/family to ensure all steps of the expatriation process are clear. To do this,

Barclays has an International Assignments Services (IAS) team that supports the HRBP, the line manager of both home and host country, and the individual employee. The IAS team is located within key global regions and is in a strong position to provide key financial and cost data to all parties, and help facilitate the move once agreed.

The HRBP in the host and home country will track the employee while on assignment and ensure the employee is kept up to date with key information, and to ensure the key skills obtained on assignment are captured for talent and succession plan purposes. At the end of the assignment the HRBP will work with the business and individual to secure either a role back in the home country, an extension to the current assignment or an alternative assignment.

Culture awareness modules and profiles

Another key priority for the HR function is to define and support a global mindset among the senior leadership team. As the business continues on a dynamic growth curve, the business reflects a more global than a European focus. Two key initiatives have been developed to help and support the senior leadership team lead and embed a global culture.

The first is awareness-building among the senior leadership community. A series of workshop modules have been created to help facilitate the understanding of the cultures that Barclaycard International work in or potentially could expand into in the near future. The workshops have been based on creating an extensive range of country profiles through external research, knowledge from Barclaycard's employees and the support from the IAS team. The workshops will help raise each individual's understanding of their own personal behaviours and will help each employee understand in greater detail the cultural challenges faced in each country.

The second is building cross-cultural training interventions. These may include taster sessions run by nationals or returning employees who have been working in the country concerned. The key is to link the activities successfully into the global induction programme. In addition, personal development can be guided towards areas that will add real global value (for instance, language courses).

Talent acquisition and development

The international resourcing challenge is supported by talent management tools and techniques. Many of these processes operate at Barclays Group level, and there is significant potential for movement between international banking operations in Barclays and Barclaycard International. Talent is categorised as a priority for Barclaycard International, to concentrate on developing talent in top leadership roles, moving then from those with the potential for a handful of senior cross-Barclays roles through to those with the potential to reach the top 450 leadership roles, and then to a broader population with business talent. Over last four years Barclaycard has evolved the identification of talent. In addition to looking for both potential and performance, the 'wow' factors have been included. Integrity and performance are minimum requirements for those rated, as organisations often see succession planning and talent identification as separate processes, but in Barclays they are increasingly integrated and long-term incentives are tied to the capabilities identified.

Internally, HRBPs facilitate twice-yearly reviews of talent, agree who is on the talent plan and agree with the business the development opportunities open to them. This could vary from courses to development roles in other cultures. They have fairly robust information about who has done what, where, and with what desires for international mobility. Where they do not have the skills in place, they aim to move people into arenas that will develop these skills.

Externally, Barclaycard uses the top grading approach to hiring senior leaders. The role of the HRBP and the business is to find the top 10% of candidates in their field of expertise on a global basis, known as 'A' players. In addition, candidates are required to have an international mindset. Alignment with Barclaycard values is important, and candidates need to have a history of international working and, given the nature of the sector, need to have been involved in stretching roles, such as international mergers and acquisitions. However, when resourcing rapid international expansion, do you start to recruit people now for the markets that you want to move into, or do you wait until you are in-market or near-market? The challenge is to 'resource ahead of the curve'. One of the approaches taken at Barclaycard International is to invest in market-mapping. This has been done in domestic markets for a while, but they now use research agencies and headhunters to map a wider range of geographical labour markets by researching the people working in roles similar to the ones that will be needed.

Global policies and frameworks

Global policies and frameworks are required to ensure consistency, rigour, global governance and risk management; however, these are challenging, given the cultural, legal and social environments.

Barclaycard International operates its global processes on an exception basis – such that even if the activity is culturally uncomfortable, the policies establish explicit guidance and global protocols that make it clear what must be done, unless it is illegal to do so.

There are a number of group-wide global standards to which Barclaycard International must adhere. One such example is the new global pre-employment screening policy, a subset of the global resourcing policy. With the increasing need for control monitoring processes to be well established (Sarbanes-Oxley compliance), Barclaycard International needs to manage its business risk by conducting rigorous levels of due diligence on potential employees. Certain requirements of the new group-framework cannot be met owing to legal constraints, and others are difficult to meet owing to local cultural and social constraints that cannot be ignored.

Conclusion

Barclaycard International has a challenging and rapid growth strategy. If it is to be as successful as its stated ambition, the need for a truly global approach to doing business will become ever more apparent. In support of this, the HR function has an exciting, interesting and challenging agenda to deliver in the next few years.

ENDNOTE

1 This case study is based on interviews with: Wendy Meikle, HR Director Barclaycard International; Jo Green, HR Business Partner; Vanessa Mastral, HR Business Partner Spain; Corina Pick, Manager Human Resources Germany; Aoife McAuliffe, HR Business Partner Ireland; and Andy MacDonald, HR Business Partner.

MECHANISMS FOR GLOBAL CONSISTENCY IN RECRUITMENT, SELECTION AND ASSESSMENT

8

❖ **The three most common 'super-ordinate' themes that organisations use to provide consistency to their people management practices**

Having discussed a couple of issues where local cultural sensitivity comes to the fore, we can return to the need for global consistency. In practice, global HRM seems to revolve around the ability of the organisation to find a concept that has 'relevance' to managers across several countries – despite the fact that they have different values embedded in different national cultures and despite the reality that these global themes may end up being operationalised with some local adaptation. The corporate strategy is usually expressed through performance management systems applied globally that measure and manage a balanced series of outcomes that must be achieved. However, organisations also use some *super-ordinate themes* to provide a degree of consistency to their people management worldwide, and as an attempt to socialise employee behaviour and action.

The most common super-ordinate themes in the process of globalising HR are:

1   core strategic competencies that are considered to differentiate the firm and lead to its competitive advantage. These are usually reflected in a series of organisational capabilities or competencies that, once specified, are integrated into career development and/or performance management systems[1]

2   the pursuit of talent management initiatives

3   corporate and global brands, whereby organisations think about their external brand image and corporate reputation, and the ways in which their employees identify with and actively support the brand.[2]

Each of these brings its own challenges when managed on the global stage and is considered in turn in the following chapters.

ENDNOTES

1   Sparrow, P.R. (1997) Organisational competencies: creating a strategic behavioural framework for selection and assessment, in N. Anderson and P. Herriot (eds) *International Handbook of Selection and Assessment.* Chichester: John Wiley, 343–68

2   See for example: Harris, F. and de Chernatony, L. (2001) Corporate branding and corporate brand performance, *European Marketing Journal* Vol. 35, Nos. 3–4. 441–56; Davies, G., Chun, R. Da Silva, R.V. and Roper, S. (2003) *Corporate Reputation and Competitiveness.* London: Routledge.

❖ **Key HR processes are central to managing talent and assisting international mobility**

❖ **Single-competency models do not map easily from one culture to another, even within Europe**

Changes in the way that international businesses organise themselves and the desire to harmonise more operations on a pan-national basis have seen the growth of global competency models. Those organisations using a competency-based approach to recruitment internationally can draw on the comfort that the use of competencies is still in vogue and appears to be still expanding globally. A survey by the World Federation of Personnel Management Associations shows a small increase in the use of competencies from 2000 to 2004.[1] Some organisations are integrating their HR around global capabilities.

> '...the use of competencies is still in vogue and appears to be still expanding globally.'

In order to manage talent and foster more international mobility, key HR processes that are intended to help build the organisation's capability are being brought together. This is leading to more co-ordinated management of external resourcing, talent benchmarking, deployment decision forums, high-potential review processes, a focus on reward and recognition in order to link individual performance, development and reward more closely with performance, and development partnering or coaching.

KEY QUESTIONS

As a consequence, more organisations are using assessment centres for external recruitment, or launching international development centres for internal assessment, benchmarked against single-competency models. This raises two key questions:

❖ Is it possible or legitimate to define a single set of competencies for use across international borders?

❖ Can people from different cultures be accurately assessed against them?

Received wisdom tells us that at a very high level of generalisation this is possible – and indeed is being done by most large organisations. However, experience also shows that there are links between cultural background and people's perceptions of what good performance looks like (and by implication, therefore, the sorts of competencies that will be identified and will be seen as legitimate to assess). In short, considerable caution needs to be exerted when attempting to recruit to a single-competency model derived in one dominant culture but being applied to applicants from another. Evidence for this view comes from a number of sources:

1   The organisational sociologists have shown convincingly that there are very different national business systems that operate even within a single region such as Europe. Work that has examined 'how managers are made' (that is, the vocational education and training systems that forge their competence, the ways in which they are socialised into the organisation, the different emphases of internal management development systems etc) shows that still within Europe there are at least four competing management models: the Anglo-Saxon model; the French model; the Germanic model; and the Scandinavian model. These models are associated with very different assumptions about relevant competencies.[2] This is reflected, for example, in the skills and competencies assessed (or not) at point of entry into the organisation, different competencies listed in job adverts across countries for the same sorts of job, differences in what managers have to do to be considered as high-flyers, and so forth. An interesting case study demonstrating this was the Transmanche-link.[3]

2   Similarly, case studies of the use of competency models on a global basis also reveal the ways in which they have to be adapted when used for more diverse populations. For example, one of the first organisations to use competency models as a central design feature of its global HR strategy was BP with its Project 1990. When this was examined to see how it could be adapted to operate globally, it was clear that:

the competencies were capable of cross-cultural implementation and represented a cogent statement of the shift in management behaviour required. However, the behavioural anchors used to describe specific competencies were in some instances unnecessarily directive and contained a culturally provocative bias ... competencies were capable of crossing cultural barriers in their essential meaning and purpose (reinforcing their use as a 'corporate glue' to integrate human resource policies and practices) but also that their implementation and assessment would require greater effort in order to customise and translate the behavioural indicators to fit the culturally different groups involved. The customisation process, however, had to avoid any misinterpretation or fundamental change to the meaning of the competencies.[4]

A recent study by consultants and work psychologists looking at global organisations such as Marconi, Nestlé and the food division of Unilever shows that such differences still persist. It concluded:

Although it should be possible to design competencies that have cross-cultural validity, subtle important differences of perception concerning individual behaviours frequently mean that direct comparisons between candidates from specific countries are subject to systematic bias ... when using the assessment centre technique, systematic differences should be expected between the behaviour of people from different countries as they strive to meet different mental models of what good performance looks like ... [do not] assume that any competency is universally applicable just because a company has included it in its corporate competency framework.[5]

'...there are scores of different, culturally embedded models of effective leadership across cultures.'

The material at the beginning of this report on global leadership models reaffirms this view. It showed that there are scores of different, culturally embedded models of effective leadership across cultures. Reflecting all these views, most leading organisations apply a series of pragmatic 'work-arounds' to ensure that the essence of the systems is kept intact across their international operations, but that there is scope for 'reasonable variation' and 'flexibility'.

ENSURING FLEXIBILITY IN THE ASSESSMENT OF GLOBAL COMPETENCIES

A recent examination of global staffing policies in Agilent Technologies, Dow Chemical Company, IBM, Motorola, Proctor and Gamble, and Shell Oil concluded that these organisations:[6]

- understood that philosophies generalise, but administrative details do not
- standardise *what* is assessed (intent, principles and guidelines) but allow flexibility in *how* it is assessed
- allow for the same competencies to be measured in different ways (that is, vary the use of assessment centres, psychological tests etc) while still maintaining a global standard.

As one goes down the level of detail in any common HR process (for example, who conducts the interview, whether pre-screens are by telephone or in person, which particular tests are used in which particular country etc) the set of universals becomes less.

Where local and non-standard elements of the assessment still exist for pragmatic reasons, their weighting in central resourcing decisions against other elements can be reduced.

In order to make the necessary 'work-around' judgements, these organisations needed to have:

- trained people with the experience to assess the legitimacy of local variations and make decisions or choices
- effective networks and teams to which the responsibility had been assigned to make such decisions and then pass the logic of each decision on to other operating countries.

As the above research shows, the use of specific tools and techniques needs to come hand in hand with consideration of issues involving appropriateness across cultures, the existence and ease of translation, the availability of norms across countries, and the ability of key suppliers and vendors of relevant services themselves to operate on a global basis. These sorts of consideration are outlined in the concluding section on local sensitivity issues (see Chapter 13).

ENDNOTES

1 Worldlink (2005) Competencies still in vogue, new survey shows. *Worldlink*. Vol. 15, No. 2. 1.

2 See Sparrow, P.R. and Hiltrop, J. (1994) *European human resource management in transition*. London: Prentice-Hall for an overview of all this material.

3 See for example: Winch, G.M., Clifton, N and Millar, C. (2000) Organisation and management in an Anglo-French consortium: the case of the Transmanche-link. *Journal of Management Studies*. Vol. 37, No. 5. 663–85.

4 Sparrow, P.R. and Bognanno, M. (1993) Competency requirement forecasting: issues for international selection and assessment. *International Journal of Selection and Assessment*. Vol. 1, No. 1. 50–4. 53.

5   Milsom, J. (2004) The growing importance of cross-cultural
    assessment. *Competency and Emotional Intelligence*. Vol. 11, No. 4.
    19–22.

6   Ryan, A.M., Wiechmann, D. and Hemingway, M. (2003) Designing
    and implementing global staffing systems: Part II. Best practices.
    Human Resource Management. Vol. 42, No. 1. 85–94.

INTERNATIONAL TALENT MANAGEMENT

10

* **Definitions, and the importance, of talent management within centralised and decentralised organisations**

* **Market-mapping is a significant aid to helping recruit 'ahead of the curve'**

* **Both commercial and not-for-profit organisations need to work more closely with national teams**

In a similar manner to global capability systems, talent management processes can also be used to bring a degree of consistency to international resourcing decisions. Unlike the use of competencies, however, where there is a strong corporate culture, the use of talent management approaches can often be easier to harmonise across countries. In part this is because many talent management systems have a focus on a series of underlying core values that are strongly reflective of the corporate and industry culture, and therefore more easily seen as being universal. In this section:

* some basic principles of talent management are introduced

* some new developments in tools and techniques are noted

* the context for the fourth and last case study is introduced.

> '...the use of talent management approaches can often be easier to harmonise across countries.'

Talent management was an important part of the Barclaycard International case study but many of the principles apply to other sectors too. The Save the Children case study (see Chapter 11) also looks at the challenge of talent management in a context of devolving responsibility for international recruitment to the line.

THE PURPOSES OF TALENT MANAGEMENT

Talent management has been defined as an integrated set of corporate initiatives aimed at improving the calibre, availability and flexible utilisation of exceptionally capable (high-potential) employees who can have a disproportionate impact on organisational performance.[1] The purpose of a successful talent management system is to attract, retain, develop and utilise employees in ways that create:

* sustainable commercial competitiveness through the alignment of employee competence, behaviours and intellectual energy with business activity

* higher levels of focused innovation

* improved staff engagement and commitment

* lower loss rates of knowledge and experience

* lower external resourcing costs.

Talent management is important in both centralised and decentralised international organisations. A study of 30 UK organisations drew attention to the importance of senior management development activity, succession planning and the development of an international cadre of managers:

> [There is a] growing recognition that the success of international business depends most importantly on the quality of top executive talent and how effectively these critical resources are managed and developed.[2]

However, talent management on a global basis is a far broader concept than plotting a series of international assignments for young high-potentials and an international cadre of managers. When global lines of business are introduced, there is a more immediate relationship between the International HR professional and the global leadership teams within major business functions or markets. Many organisations conduct various 'calibrations' of talent on a global basis in order to plan business development. International organisations want to know who their top people are and what the key roles are within the business that they need these people for. They want to know how they can develop people, get them to key positions, and build succession cover for these key positions. They have to develop a much deeper level of understanding about the links between the business agenda and the capabilities of the most talented people in the organisation, and also understand the potential for mobility around these people.

> '...talent management on a global basis is a far broader concept than plotting a series of international assignments for young high-potentials...'

This challenge inevitably leads organisations to think about talent on a more global basis. There has been a fairly common response to the challenge, which has included:

❖ researching into 'consumer insights' with current and potential employees, sister companies, external agencies, and benchmarking with external companies

❖ managing the 'talent pipeline' – trying to recruit 'ahead of the curve' instead of the more traditional vacancy-based recruitment

❖ communicating an awareness in graduate schools and businesses to get the people they need

❖ developing internal talent pools around the world

❖ creating skilled and competent teams of assessors in different regional geographies

❖ managing recruitment suppliers on a global basis, introducing speed, cost and quality controls, establishing master contracts to co-ordinate the messages conveyed and the use of preferred partners, and ensuring audit trails to protect against legal issues associated with global diversity

❖ e-enabling jobs noticeboards, and redesigning websites to convey important messages about the employer brand.

Organisations are using a number of strategic tools to help manage talent on a global basis. The CIPD globalisation research noted that the use of these tools has led to much more joint work between the HR function and marketing and corporate communication functions. The development of an employment brand and identification of an employee value proposition on a global basis, the tracking of associated employee engagement data, and concern for corporate social responsibility are all examples where marketing input might be sought.

Another recent development is the use of market-mapping techniques. This was seen, for example, in the Barclaycard International case, where the business model is able to identify the countries/markets that will be developed next, and so some advance research into those labour markets becomes possible. It forms part of the armoury of techniques to help organisations recruit 'ahead of the curve'.

STRATEGIC TALENT MANAGEMENT TOOLS: MARKET-MAPPING

In the same way that organisations examine local business partners when they intend to move into a particular business market, they need to understand the situation in the labour market. A number of consulting firms claim to be able to combine intelligence gathered as a result of local sourcing campaigns, industry networking and direct market-mapping activity to be able to carry out an 'opportunity analysis' of any specific international labour market.

Frequently an HR function only has a very short time to find out the extent of talent in any new labour market, and so the ability to speed up the collection of intelligence or to forewarn a project team on potential resourcing issues can be important. High-level skills may be hard to locate or rare on the ground, with implications for the use of domestic talent and expatriation policies. In the same vein, there may only be a small pool of candidates in a target country who in the interests of employer branding need to be 'educated' and informed about the organisation through targeted events and a managed communication strategy for that country.

Market-mapping is an umbrella term, and services range from informing succession plans through to virtual benchmarking of talent, and analyses of competitors' products and services, structures and associated role knowledge and breadth, team sizes, star performers and market image. Market-mapping seems to be most attractive to organisations when they are:

❖ seeking high-level technical or business-facing skills in a new international labour market, that is, situations where the 'intellectual capital' owned by potential employees can be an important success factor to any international project

❖ wanting to set up operations in a new country but do not wish their competitors to be aware of this intention.

In these situations, the advance investment in research, intelligence and branding might be seen to pay off. Most certainly there is a demand for HR professionals with these skills, with job adverts asking for people with: strong professional networks within a specific industry segment; connections to a community of expertise in that segment; insights into innovative recruitment and attraction strategies, building talent pipelines and helping to directly source candidates through headhunting; and solid knowledge of the relevant employment legislation in any particular country or region.

It can often be assumed that such practices are the preserve of large multinationals and that the practices and experiences of not-for-profit organisations in the international management area are very different from those of large private sector firms. However, there are probably more similarities than differences these days, although of course the financial resources that might be devoted to talent management strategies are more constrained. Charities have often thought that they must learn from the corporate sector, but in reality this learning is now a two-way process. There are a number of common issues experienced across these sectors.

Historically, the emphasis in international recruitment, selection and assessment has been on recruiting and training expatriates to work with national teams. But it is now important in both private sector and not-for-profit organisations to expand and build on working relationships with national teams more, ensuring that both the HR systems and the candidates recruited create space in the management of the organisation to give voice to national management, for example, including national teams in the induction of expatriate staff by preparing not only the expatriate to cope with cultural differences, but also the national teams. In the same vein, matching the capability of the organisation across all of its geographical operations with the skills that are available in the local labour market frequently reveals skills shortages in both sectors.

> 'Organisations have to be more creative in how they resource international employees...'

Organisations have to be more creative in how they resource international employees — they have to take more risks as they experiment with candidates from untried labour pools. The

balance of attention given to different parts of the recruitment and selection process may need to be changed. If the person specification cannot be met in all its elements during the recruitment process, induction and training processes might be strengthened to compensate for this and build the required capability.

There are some areas of international management where the experience base in the not-for-profit sector is more developed. Attention has been drawn recently to the need for organisations to ensure their talent management processes also establish diversity at senior levels in the organisation.[3] This is not just for ethical reasons, but is increasingly underpinned by such business and operational logics as:

❖ the need for not just front-line staff but also the top tier of the organisation to match its customer or user base, in order that meaningful and more effective strategies are considered

❖ the international scarcity of many advanced and specialised skills that are central to the success of large-scale and cross-organisation projects.

ENDNOTES

1 Smilansky, J. (2004) *The Systematic Management of Executive Talent.* London: CIPD.

2 Scullion, H. and Starkey, K. (2000) In search of the changing role of the corporate human resource function in the international firm, *International Journal of Human Resource Management.* Vol. 11, No. 6. 1061–81. 1065.

3 Arkin, A. (2005) Hidden talents. *People Management.* Vol. 11, No. 15. 26–30.

DEVOLVING RESPONSIBILITY FOR INTERNATIONAL RECRUITMENT

11

❖ **Save the Children is moving more and more towards a decentralised focus on national-level advocacy**

❖ **International staff are recruited by countries rather than by the London HQ**

❖ **Selection techniques and talent management are both becoming more sophisticated**

Not-for-profit organisations have perhaps had to learn more quickly how to combine diversity priorities with talent management processes. They have, however, also had to change many of the practices that were once traditional to their sector. The fourth and final case study, below, illustrates the emerging international recruitment, selection and assessment strategy of Save the Children UK as it has sought to decentralise responsibility for international recruitment.

CHANGING INTERNATIONAL RESOURCING PRACTICES AT SAVE THE CHILDREN UK[1]

Save the Children UK has a mission to 'fight for children in the UK and around the world who suffer from poverty, disease, injustice and violence and to work with them to find lifelong answers to the problems they face'. In its activities, emergency relief runs alongside long-term development and prevention work.

The organisation works across six geographical regions, each managing a wide range of activities. For example, in East and Southern Africa Save the Children UK works in nine countries. Programmes include promoting child rights and child participation, protecting children in emergencies, child-focused economic policies, health and nutrition, food security and livelihoods, emergency preparedness and delivering food aid in humanitarian crises.

In South and Central Asia it works in seven countries – Afghanistan, Bangladesh, India, Kyrgyzstan, Pakistan, Sri Lanka and Tajikistan. In Sri Lanka it had staff on the ground when the earthquake and tsunami struck on 26

December 2004. In the short term, these staff had to respond quickly with food, water, medicine and shelter to assist thousands of children and their families, launch major efforts to register and reunify separated or unaccompanied children with their families and create safe areas for displaced children.

In the initial phase of the emergency, Save the Children supported the distribution of relief family packs containing food, basic medical supplies and other non-food items to over 25,000 families in the worst-affected areas. Subsequently, they provided safe opportunities for children to learn and play, as well as support for the Sri Lankan government's attempts to get all children back to school as quickly as possible.

Different categories of employee

Save the Children recruits to opportunities in three different categories: long-term development posts based overseas; emergency posts based overseas; and locally appointed posts based in the UK and countries where it works. Candidates are subject to host-country requirements. For example, in some countries a work permit and (rarely) an HIV test is required as part of the visa application. Typically, there is a large response to vacancies, although around three-quarters can usually be screened out owing to the applicant's not meeting the person specification. Save the Children is working on a number of measures to enable it to attract and recruit talent to its worldwide roles.

Over the last few years, Save the Children has been repositioning itself and looking at its long-term strategy. It has launched a new brand positioning statement and confirmed a new strategic direction, focusing on national-level advocacy. It has decentralised its operations and devolved more accountability to line managers to support this focus. It has also defined four key objective areas for the organisation:

1   reducing childhood death and sickness

2   children having a basic education

3   children having enough to eat

4   protecting children from exploitation and abuse.

The impact on international recruitment

These developments have affected recruitment in a number of ways:

❖   devolvement of HR responsibility to the line, leaving a smaller, more strategic, global head-office HR function

❖   changes in the skill specification for international appointments

❖   developments to improve the sophistication of the selection process

❖   more attention to the employer brand

❖   focusing of talent management processes on creating a cadre of internationally mobile staff on permanent contracts in whom the organisation can invest and have a longer-term relationship, and building the capacity and careers of national staff.

In the last few years there has been a significant shift in the structure and culture of the organisation, with associated changes in the nature of its international management. HR has recently been devolved, with more authority being given to country senior management teams.

As part of the restructuring, the HR team at headquarters was reduced in size, becoming less operational and providing a central source of expertise, which includes a specialist international resourcing team. This will allow country and regional teams to get on with the day-to-day work at field level and allow the resourcing team at HQ to concentrate on developing more creative and co-ordinated recruitment support and initiatives.

The global resourcing team has a head of global resourcing, a resourcing manager and a resourcing systems manager. In the first few weeks of its existence, the team prepared a resourcing toolkit and commenced the first of a series of workshops in London for country-based HR managers. The training included strategies and key steps in recruiting international staff, which is now done by the countries rather than a London-based team.

The global HR team has to: understand the different labour markets that Save the Children sources candidates from; understand the organisation's competitors for talent and best practice globally, in order to advise line managers on the best resourcing strategies; and lead the organisation in developing its resourcing capability. New regional HR managers will also play an important part in international recruitment, acting as the 'eyes and ears' of the organisation at a local level, spotting internal talent, understanding the local recruitment media and helping to build up databases of potential employees. Induction is a costly process, and many staff in the sector move out of an organisation to return later on another programme. Save the Children is looking to address this by re-evaluating its retention strategies and expanding its candidate networks.

Sharing best practice

It is important to ensure that best practice and learning about recruitment is available to field staff. A 'recruitment planner' has been developed for use whenever a new assignment is started. This aids setting the resourcing strategy, including identifying the likely whereabouts of suitable candidates and appropriate ways to market the role. It is also important to track talented employees, both while they work for the organisation and when they are engaged elsewhere. Networking skills are important for the HR function, especially where they seek people for specialist functions such as food security, child protection or nutrition. There is no overabundance of well-qualified candidates.

As charities like Save the Children compete with each other for these staff, agencies are increasingly recognising the need to grow more talent for the sector either individually or in co-operation. Save the Children has recently developed a child protection trainee scheme to assist resourcing in this difficult specialist area. Six trainees were recruited to the programme in 2005. They will rotate through different programmes over a 12-month period and are each assigned to an individual mentor. Save the Children UK is looking to work with its sister organisation Save the Children US on further 'grow your own' schemes.

Job descriptions used to be lengthy but are now much slicker, with a more focused person specification. Traditionally, considerable weight was given to technical skills and previous overseas humanitarian or development experience, even for more general management roles. While technical skills are still required for specialist roles, such as programme directors and programme managers, the emphasis is much more on good management skills. These general managers have to supervise other specialists, and candidates must demonstrate that they have effective capacity-building and performance management skills.

Other selection criteria include relevant experience in a developing country (usually two years), an understanding of development issues, teamworking skills, coaching and training skills, analytical and planning skills, cultural sensitivity, the ability to adapt to new living and working environments, and language skills where appropriate. Performance management and accountability are weighted particularly heavily.

Changing sources of recruitment

Staff are now sourced from a broader range of backgrounds, and better links are being forged with the corporate sector. Candidates from sectors that have not been used before, such as the military, finance, sales and marketing, are now being seen in final candidate pools. The organisation is better prepared to take risks with candidates from different sectors and counterbalance this by giving more attention to induction, learning and development and evaluation.

The organisation relies less now on newspapers as a recruitment medium and more on the web. Without the same resources that large, private sector firms may be able to employ, HR staff have to be more focused in their approach. For example, in a recent campaign, skills shortages were experienced in one of the Francophone countries, the Democratic Republic of Congo (DRC). In addition to the usual humanitarian websites frequently used to source employees, a campaign was run on French websites and an executive search conducted. The search firm was also commissioned to undertake a study on where francophone candidates typically look and why Save the Children staff enjoy working in the region. The firm concluded that Save the Children were seen by candidates as being very UK-centric. Hence all adverts for this country are now also run in French.

Recruitment still relies a lot on the overall brand and image of the organisation, and Save the Children ensures that all advertising, including HR advertising, fits with the brand and portrays strong, positive messages about what being part of the Save the Children team is all about. Online recruitment is a powerful tool for international resourcing. In this sector, speed is everything, particularly when an emergency hits, as NGOs are competing for the same high-calibre candidates. Appointments have to be marketed more strongly now, with attention being given to key selling-points of working in a particular programme, country or region and the difference Save the Children can make. This requires more customised advertising. E-resourcing capability is being reviewed to ensure it is fast and effective and can be accessed at a local as well as global level.

In parallel with this, selection techniques have become more formalised. Psychometrics are now used more often, designed to assess specific competencies. This means that the issue of using tests on a global basis across cultures has to be understood.

The role of values

Values are important and cut across recruitment activity. Save the Children's values, as emphasised in its public materials, are being child-focused, ambitious but practical, independent, open, collaborative, accountable and working as a team. Common to the whole charity sector, employees have to be accountable to trustees and justify to the public and institutional donors where money is spent. Being accountable is expressed as being responsible to those the organisation exists to serve – children, and their families and communities, as well as those that support its work. For Save the Children employees, this means that professionally they have to be sound, scrupulous, efficient and effective. Selection methods contain a number of checks to deter and detect those who might put children at risk.

Talent management processes

Talent management processes are also becoming more sophisticated. A new scheme called the International Core Team has just been launched in 2006. This is an internal talent scheme that aims to establish a longer-term relationship with international staff, enabling them to build their expertise and global perspectives and, through this, improve organisational effectiveness for children. Team members are offered a permanent contract with the expectation that they will move to a new country posting every three to five years. In support of this concept will be much more attention to skills development and career-planning for team members. Work is also being done to develop more opportunities for national staff to move into international roles through helping them to gain the international perspectives required.

Looking forward, more work is expected to be done around the employer brand, incorporating it into resourcing strategies in a way that brings the brand to life. The developments in global resourcing being made will be fitted together as part of an integrated strategy. Save the Children is also looking more at how it works with volunteers and uses their skills on a global basis, including volunteer secondments from some of its corporate sponsors. Policies and practices are being reviewed around this, with a view to linking work in with recruitment strategies being developed, as well as candidate databases being built.

Save the Children has given all line managers responsibility for national recruitment, passing the entire recruitment process down to 40 country directors. The Head of Global Resourcing argues that:

We wanted to concentrate on national-level advocacy and give country managers much more accountability with the appropriate resources, so it made sense for them to own everything about their country programme.[2]

This devolution has gone hand-in-hand with a shift to more strategic HR management at the centre, including more standardised and simplified job descriptions, management of a core of internationally mobile staff and investigation of the employment brand.

A significant challenge for global organisations in terms of initiating their hunt for talent is to decide what the overriding message to talented people is, both in terms of 'who they are' as an organisation and also 'what they stand for'. This moves us on to a discussion of employer branding in the context of international recruitment, selection and assessment.

ENDNOTES

1 The Save the Children case is based on interviews and discussions with Elaine Sullivan, International HR Manager, and Rachel Westcott, Head of Resourcing. Additional commentary and background data has been provided by Martha Newman, S. Parsons, L. Bedelian and Z. Davies.

2 Czerny, A. (2006) Save the Children hands over recruitment to line managers. *People Management.* Vol. 12, No. 6. 12.

EMPLOYER BRANDING AND INTERNATIONAL RECRUITMENT

12

❖ **Discovering why good employees should stay with their employer involves looking at all major HR policies and practices**

❖ **Finding a balance between the central planning and the local knowledge that has to underpin the strategies**

❖ **Does the creation of a common employer brand across international operations make sense?**

❖ **Different countries 'buy in' to the employer brand to markedly differing degrees**

There has been much debate in the profession about the management of employer brands internationally. It is an important challenge for many large international organisations. Employer branding – the image of the organisation as seen through the eyes of *external* stakeholders – represents an extension of brand management and is another development whereby HR thinking has been influenced by that of the marketing function. Building or defending the corporate brand or reputation has become a major concern in many industries. Employer branding requires consistency and uniformity in delivering the brand identity by all *internal* stakeholders, including employees. However, currently, we still know little about the linkages between HR and marketing in the brand management process, despite increasing awareness that the HR function is now becoming involved in this work on an international scale.

> '...we still know little about the linkages between HR and marketing in the brand management process...'

THE CHALLENGE OF CREATING AN AUTHENTIC BRAND

For global organisations, this involves constantly re-selling the proposition to employees as to why their organisation is the one for which they should work and delivering the promised experience in practice. The challenge then is to understand what makes a really good person want to stay with them *globally*. The answer tends to affect both the development of people, which is a key driver of retention, and how the organisation recruits. It

affects how the organisation approaches the media, how it conducts its investor relations, how it designs compensation and benefits, and how it designs performance management systems. In other words, it informs all the policies and procedures.

These messages cannot be aspirational – they have to be grounded in what the organisation really offers and what potential employees really want. The processes must back up what the organisation says it is. The key messages to potential employees must also make sense in all the organisation's markets worldwide. The organisation has to pick out which messages they can match and where they are able to give out a message that can be fulfilled. Each market has cultural differences, but also similarities.

> 'Each market has cultural differences, but also similarities.'

A number of organisations today devote considerable resources to the creation of a global employer brand. For example, in 2002, immediately after the merger of SmithKline Beecham and Glaxo Wellcome, GlaxoSmithKline (GSK) initiated a global research process to help it define its employer brand and improve its recruitment processes.[1] Opinions as to what the organisation meant varied by location, function and legacy company culture. Seventy focus groups were run across 20 locations to reveal common sources of pride and a 'corporate signature' that could subsequently feature on all of the organisation's marketing materials (the 'Together we can make life better' campaign). Guidelines were developed for copy-writing, image usage and layout. The brand was first established in the USA and UK, and was then marketed across Europe and the Asia Pacific region.

EMPLOYER BRANDING STRATEGIES

A recent study has analysed the aims and strategies of 236 organisations in 11 countries from the financial services, consulting, healthcare, manufacturing, retail and telecommunications sectors.[2] The commonest objectives for employer branding work are to enhance the appeal of the employer among potential employees and to secure long-term recruitment needs. To a lesser extent, the aim is also to create internal pride and commitment and fulfil short-term recruitment needs. It is an externally focused strategy. Most of the information that organisations seek in order to develop a brand are, however, internal – knowledge and experience of their organisation, internal surveys of employees – with some external analysis of the labour market. Strategies centre around articulating an overall recruitment and retention approach, defining core values for the employer, refining and aligning recruitment processes and planned communication material.

Around one-fifth of organisations believe they have a very clear employer value proposition, an equal number do not believe so, and around one-half feel this can be further developed. Measurement and evaluation are mainly based on levels of employee satisfaction and turnover, and to a lesser extent external employer attraction, total number of applications, employee loyalty and the time needed to fill vacancies. The majority of people involved have HR backgrounds, but the larger the organisation, the more likely it is that specialists work in marketing and communications, and they are becoming more involved in general. Control still tends to be at an operational level. Some 30% of organisations plan to increase their investments in this area (average investments are €140 per employee per year) and, 60% will maintain current investment levels.

LESSONS FROM ACROSS THE CASE STUDIES

However, judging from the four case studies in this study and related discussions at CIPD events, an important learning point for many organisations that have dealt with employer branding issues on an international basis is that they develop over time. Perhaps reflecting the internal focus noted above, initially attention has to be given to 'stabilising' key people management processes across different geographical operations. Once this has been done, decisions can then be made about the look and consistency of the employer brand. Some early and basic considerations include the following:

- ❖ creating the same physical brand – for example the logo and literature

- ❖ sharing a common mission, vision and set of stated values

- ❖ setting minimum HR standards and conditions to shape the nature of employee engagement

- ❖ examining how the pay strategy and associated benchmarks define the calibre of applicants

- ❖ understanding how this helps bring consistency to the employee experience in terms of competencies and leadership capability.

The first issue is often fairly easy to address. The answer often lies within the business strategy and the reasons it provides as to why the organisation is now operating in a particular international labour market. However, once the need for a common physical brand has been established, more subtle judgements often have to be made.

The second issue, sharing mission, vision and stated values, is again easy to initiate (although in practice extremely hard to bring about). However, attention is given to communicating these consistently through the various programmes and media. It is generally important that performance management and development processes are made the same across all countries as early as possible, given the impact these have on mission, vision and values. Adjustments to these processes inevitably have to be made for local cultural and legal reasons.

> 'HR professionals often point out that…international operations can be very variable in terms of their adherence to standards and procedures.'

The third issue requires more international collaboration in HR. HR professionals often point out that – certainly in the area of recruitment – international operations can be very variable in terms of their adherence to standards and procedures. Again, before more strategic considerations may be made, there is a need to set minimum standards for the conduct of HR. This generally requires joint input from in-country HR partners and central oversight. Without the confidence that key HR processes are conducted to a common standard, it is then difficult to integrate employee experiences and engagement with the mission, strategy and values. Engagement scores on key 'tracker' opinion survey items might just reflect poor execution of HR, rather than any more fundamental problem with the employer brand. Organisations either need to establish pan-international frameworks to ensure that policies and practices across countries are harmonised or that there is a direct 'read across' between countries from one policy to another.

The fourth and fifth issues are very important but are also easy to overlook. Examining how the pay strategy and associated benchmarks define the calibre of applicants, and understanding how this calibre of local applicants helps bring consistency to the employee experience (in terms of the competencies and the leadership capability they are capable of displaying), is a matter of judgement and learning. However, a local pay strategy based on lower levels of pay, for example, might mean attracting a lower calibre of manager, with the consequence that they are not as good at managing the employment relationship and creating outcomes in the operation that match the brand behaviours. Deciding how to align rewards with the realities of the local labour market can often be a source of tension in organisations as they internationalise. Much of the knowledge about rewards, markets and the impact that central pay strategy has on the local recruitment market resides in-country. But the thought leadership around the development of global standards for recruitment and rewards exists in the centre of the organisation. The two need to be matched up.

> 'Deciding how to align rewards with the realities of the local labour market can often be a source of tension in organisations...'

Managing the employer brand for international recruitment purposes often requires judgements to be made about the capability of the international operations. Given that international expansion in many organisations is on the basis of acquisitions, or through international joint ventures (IJVs), it becomes important to consider the employer brand. Organisations need to understand what makes people want to work for them in each international labour market that they recruit in. This employee value proposition (EVP) says much about the nature of the reality of the employer brand, and work has to be carried out to look at this EVP in key labour markets.

In the section on cross-national advertising, it was pointed out that organisations have to balance the need for global consistency and local responsiveness. This applies to the issue of employer branding too, where some experts believe that barriers at the local level (in terms of the need for localised marketing) will prove too big a problem to surmount. Others argue that service providers can provide international organisations with the brand and cultural consistency that they seek.

MANAGING SOME OF THE REALITIES

As already noted, organisations often decide to pursue a global theme that will affect its international recruitment – such as a common EVP, set of corporate values or employer brand. However, in practice, global HRM is often also driven by other developments that can create conflicting pressures. For example, for many organisations the process of internationalisation (and the associated need for more international recruitment) has been achieved – as remarked above – on the basis of acquisitions, mergers or IJVs. The following pragmatic issues therefore have to considered before any attempts are made to develop and manage a common employer brand:

❖ Often an international operation in an overseas operation is by definition young – perhaps only in operation for a year. Bedding down perceptions about the employer brand in the internal workforce, let alone the local labour market, is difficult in such young operations. The extent to which the organisation's values are understood and internalised will vary across the international operations, depending on the maturity of each one.

❖ The business model for any particular international operation may be driven by different cost and labour market solutions across countries. Within a single country, operations might range from, for example, a call centre through to a research

and development operation or corporate function. This pattern is different across countries.

❖ The attitudes that employees will hold towards even the need for organisational identification in the first place, let alone the need to 'live' an organisation's specific values, can be very variable and simply a reflection of the job level. The typical background and labour market history of candidates that the organisation is likely to attract in any particular country can be an important influence on the desirability of creating a common international employer brand.

> 'Employees within any country will identify differently with each element of an organisation's employer brand.'

❖ Employees within any country will identify differently with each element of an organisation's employer brand. An employer brand often requires that employees adopt values that may in practice reflect group-level or 'corporate values', values associated with different 'product divisions', and values that are associated with the 'service brand'. Expecting alignment across all these different elements of an employer brand in all countries in which the organisation recruits may be unrealistic.

Such considerations are important in helping to decide whether the creation of a common employer brand across international operations makes sense. If the answer is yes, then there are a number of other decisions that often have to be made:

❖ When should an international joint venture or acquisition take on the employer brand in its fullest sense (above and beyond physical branding), and in what sequence should the HR issues that this invokes be addressed?

❖ What do the employee opinion scores, engagement data, the employee relations history and capability data suggest about the operation?

❖ What is the EVP of the potential target organisation? Does it need improving?

❖ What does this analysis imply for the future resourcing strategy?

UNDERSTANDING THE DRIVERS OF EMPLOYEE ENGAGEMENT ACROSS COUNTRIES

Importantly, these considerations have nothing to do with the issue of national culture and how this may affect employee values. One might expect that the national culture of the country that international recruitment is being carried out in will be a strong predictor of employee engagement. A number of service providers have begun to research this question. It is important to stress that all of the main service providers in this area have their own ways of measuring employee engagement and offer models. The following illustration is provided merely by way of example of this kind of analysis, not as any endorsement of the particular model outlined. There is a wealth of academic research on this question – though not under the banner of 'employee engagement' – that has been carried out.

> **'Understanding the factors that are driving the level of employee engagement across countries requires quite sophisticated analysis...'**

The role of recruitment and selection in ensuring a better fit between employee and corporate values is obvious, but currently there is pressure on organisations involved in international recruitment, selection and assessment to understand the 'drivers' of employee engagement in an international context. The need for organisations to understand and manage the nature of their employer brand across country and business operations – and the lessons that are emerging about how best to think about these issues – have generally been understood through the writing of case studies, presentations from professionals at professional conferences and consulting experience. In this section, some of these messages are explained. Understanding the factors that are driving the level of employee engagement across countries requires quite sophisticated analysis, and much experiential learning, across international operations. The need to carry out such analysis seems to be prevalent in those sectors that have experienced rapid internationalisation but that also need to convey common perceptions about their services or products, such as retail banking or consumer brand organisations.

DOES EMPLOYEE ENGAGEMENT DIFFER ACROSS COUNTRIES?

International Survey Research tracked 40 of its global clients from 1999 to 2002. They adopt a three-way split when discussing employee engagement:

❖ cognitive (how employees think about their company). Is there an intellectual fit between each employee and the organisation? Do employees believe in the organisation's goals and objectives? Do they intellectually support its values?

❖ affective (how employees feel about their company). Is there an emotional bond between the employee and the organisation? Does this make them proud to be a part of the organisation? Would each employee recommend the organisation as an employer?

❖ behavioural (how employees behave in relation to their company). This has two dimensions. First, do employees exert maximum effort at their work, and do they go the extra mile for the organisation? Second, do they intend to stay with the organisation through its successes and its setbacks?

It is argued that all three elements have to be in place in order for an employee to be engaged. ISR ran a survey of over 160,000 employees in hundreds of companies across ten countries. They analysed the relationship between growth in net income and employee engagement levels. The results of the survey showed that organisations with high levels of employee engagement outperformed the industry average over a 12-month period by 6%, while those with low levels underperformed by 9% (*www.isrsurveys.com*). They noted large international differences. On their scales – based on a composite set of eight items covering the three elements above – 75% of Brazilian or US employees are engaged, compared with 72% in the Netherlands, 70% in Australia and Canada, 67% in Germany, 66% in the UK and Singapore and 65% in Hong Kong, but only 59% in France.

They also found that different factors drove engagement in each of the countries surveyed. The type of engagement was also different across countries.

❖ In terms of what people think about their company (cognitive engagement), then US employees were most likely to believe in the goals of their company and accept the company's values, with the lowest level of engagement in France. In the UK engagement stems more from a cognitive (intellectual) engagement with their company rather than any sense of emotional attachment to its practices and purpose.

❖ In terms of emotional attachment and feelings about their company, this was highest in Brazil but lowest in Hong Kong.

❖ In terms of how employees actually act (behavioural engagement), then employees in France are least likely to put in extra discretionary effort or feel that their company inspires them to give them more, whereas US employees score highly on these questions. Employees in Brazil and the Netherlands are most likely to want to stay with their employer. Singapore, the UK, France and Australia are the countries where employees express the greatest desire to move on.

Such analyses make it clear that the specific country that an organisation is recruiting in will therefore also have an important effect on the nature of employee engagement, and hence on the value of pursuing a particular employer brand. The challenge for globalisation is, then, to align employee engagement behind the corporate values and across operations that, even within a single national culture, are likely to be recruiting from different labour markets.

ENDNOTES

1   Ford, H. (2002) World of difference. *People Management*. 27 June.
    38–40.

2   Universum (2005) *Employer Branding: Global Best Practices 2005*.
    Stockholm: Universum.

ACKNOWLEDGING THE LOCAL SELECTION AND ASSESSMENT ISSUES

13

❖ **HR business partners need a thorough knowledge of all legal and fiscal practices regarding employment in the local country**

❖ **As far as possible it is vital to achieve both global business consistency and sensitivity to national custom and practice**

❖ **To ensure consistency work needs to be done in adapting psychological and educational tests to different linguistic and cultural contexts**

The report now returns to the continuing need to ensure local sensitivity in international recruitment, selection and assessment. Given the increasing number of organisations that are conducting short-term overseas recruitment campaigns, we signal the most important issues to be aware of.

THE CHANGING ROLE OF HR BUSINESS PARTNERS

> '...the work for an HRBP is increasingly complex as organisations internationalise.'

The research shows that the challenges for the HR business partner (HRBP) vary in each country, but a common need is the question of how to ensure rigour and consistency across operations in very different cultures, business markets and labour markets. The whole HR team needs to devise frameworks that can be applied in the countries in which the organisation already has a presence, but also be aware of the countries into which the organisation *may* enter. In some sectors the business model makes it easier to be forewarned about this. However, the work for an HRBP is increasingly complex as organisations internationalise. Typically, in establishing new country operations the organisation has to:

❖ set up the legal entities to transfer employees

❖ decide what is the best mix of local recruitment

❖ investigate how local job centres should be used and build local networks

❖ assess what regionalised funding might be available from governments

❖ understand the implications and ramifications of general employment law

❖ understand specific legal frameworks (as they apply to issues such as payroll details, salary and reward factors such as contractual benefits or the value of extra work hours, contractual agreement compliance and disciplinary arrangements both in the country or to the operation of specific sectors in that country).

Sometimes these activities have to handled for a cluster of countries. During a period of rapid international expansion new countries themselves sometimes have to oversee resourcing in other start-up operations. This oversight can range from handling basic administrative work, to ensuring standards and structures, through to negotiating contractual issues and providing post-recruitment services.

HRBPs also often have to work with a range of different search agencies, from large global agencies to specialised local firms; the choice is when to use a home-country- or in-country-based agency. They have to take these agencies through an important education process, especially as regards understanding the nature of specialised skills. Given the nature of country operations, relationships with these agencies and suppliers are often handled by local HRBPs. As organisations become more international, they have to build networks across these agencies and ensure that the organisation learns both how to handle the different types of agency and understand the true global capability (or lack of it) of their suppliers, as well as the geographical spread of skills that are available in labour markets.

There may be specialist skills that exist in the home labour market but that are difficult to find in all countries (the skills may be in their infancy in local labour markets, detailed candidate searches may be expensive, local attitudes to mobility may affect the shape of the applicant pool, there may be strong regional differences in labour market behaviour). The HR function therefore has to organise itself so that it can source people from the right place. The need to source specialist skills means that organisations may look for other qualities, such as individuals who will give attention to the development of their local colleagues. The need to pass on a skill is not formally part of international roles, but just as with formal expatriates, international recruits often have to be generous in sharing their skills and transferring their knowledge.

Given the above discussion, it is clear that often considerable insight into the level of 'country capability' resides at HR partner level. HR partners, however, have to be judicious in communicating and protecting that capability while also carrying out the activities necessitated by the corporate globalisation process.

> 'An important issue...is how best to build the capability of the local operation...so that it matches the local business need.'

An important issue faced in recruiting internationally is how best to build the capability of the local operation (in terms of specialist skills) so that it matches the local business need. A key decision is which resourcing activities need strategic and central oversight, and which can be left to country-based HRBPs. Deciding and agreeing the territory and focus of new roles like this is important and sends signals to country operations about the mindset behind internationalisation.

However, once organisations get to this stage of development, an important choice is where to locate the role – in the HQ or in (any) one of the new expanding in-country bases. These decisions are bound up intimately with the identification of what the role of the HR function outside the central hub is and how country HR partners should connect back with the central hub. Implicitly, a subtle shift takes place whereby the relationship between the centre and country HR partners becomes one where the latter begins to act more like a consultant and expert on the local market, managed in the context of more globally co-ordinated initiatives.

UNDERSTANDING THE NATIONAL LEGISLATIVE CONTEXT

In-country business partners have to understand the following themselves, or be aware of the service providers who understand them:

❖ international differences in legislation affecting recruitment

❖ labour market characteristics, the impact of taxation policies on labour market behaviour, levels of skills supply, the role of regional factors in terms of mobility, and divisions on the grounds of religious, ethnic or cultural traditions

❖ cultural differences in the use of specific recruitment and selection tools and techniques.

WHERE CAN I FIND OUT MORE?

A number of research bodies, non-governmental organisations (NGOs) and professional bodies provide briefings about national legislation and HR systems. For example:

Incomes Data Services

A research organisation that is focused on employment-related areas. It has established information services covering areas ranging from employment law and pensions to developments in Europe. It publishes eight regular services on paper and in electronic format, along with research reports on important current issues in the employment field.

http://www.incomesdata.co.uk/

International Labour Organisation

The International Labour Organisation is the UN specialised agency that seeks the promotion of social justice and internationally recognised human and labour rights. It provides technical assistance primarily in the fields of: vocational training and vocational rehabilitation; employment policy; labour administration; labour law and industrial relations; working conditions; management development; co-operatives; social security; labour statistics; and occupational safety and health.

http://www.ilo.org/

Recruitment and Employment Confederation

A professional network representing the recruitment industry with 7,000 corporate members and 5,000 individual members:

http://www.rec.uk.com/rec/about-the-rec/index.aspx

In relation to differences in legislation affecting recruitment in international labour markets, the breadth of potential legislation affecting recruitment is considerable. HRBPs have to understand the law as it affects things like:

❖ use of employment exchanges and job centres

❖ outplacement

❖ temporary work

❖ fixed-term contracts

❖ hours of work

❖ time off work

❖ termination of employment

- unfair dismissal

- redundancy

- maternity leave

- discrimination and equal opportunities

- health and safety

- recruitment codes of practice

- use of psychological testing

- disclosure of information.

Moreover, HRBPs need to understand the nature or source of the law in any particular country, which ranges from codified legislation, constitutional rights, national or sectoral collective agreements, to codes of best practice that have set precedents in labour courts. After signalling the importance of understanding these differences, a couple of technical recruitment issues are briefly discussed:

- cross-national advertising

- cross-cultural psychological testing.

CROSS-NATIONAL ADVERTISING

As noted in the introduction, opinion on some issues has not changed markedly since the last report in this area, which was in 1999. Seven years ago it was noted that if the costs of getting a recruitment campaign wrong are high in the domestic market, then the potential costs of errors in global campaigns are very high. At the time, recruitment advertising service providers were operating as part of global networks in order to deliver targeted regional or global campaigns. These might have been developed in and managed from the UK, or developed for local on-ground support. Even in the early days of global recruitment campaigns it was clear that both local research skills and knowledge of culturally attuned marketing approaches was needed. Specifically, the knowledge that became important for both the recruiting organisation and the advertising consultancies was:

- local media knowledge in order to buy and place adverts that work first time

- access to local market knowledge

- advice on the content, tone and design of any advertisement to ensure sensitivity to cultural values

- translation services

- project management and co-ordination of pan-national campaigns.

The debate invariably revolves around the need to balance two aims: global consistency versus the importance of local knowledge. Awareness of national custom and practice is always important to ensure the 'cultural and creative appropriateness' of a campaign. From the advertising perspective, the most important cross-cultural differences concern:

- the role qualities associated with jobs

- the desired company qualities

- softer cultural issues such as what ideal brochures should look like, the wording of advertisements, the ability to use different forms of humour, the ability to get candidates to self-select, or not, through the communication of salaries etc.

> 'The debate invariably revolves around the need to balance two aims: global consistency versus the importance of local knowledge.'

The phrasing and design of adverts is a good example of the softer cultural issues that can be encountered. For example, in the Czech Republic language is gender-specific and it is easy to inadvertently place advertisements with obvious requests for a *reditel* (male director). Similarly, issues can be faced in Germany where the gender associated with certain words in the language can imply the sex of the preferred candidate. This is permissable under the law, but requires additional caveats to be placed in the advert clarifying equal opportunities. Awareness of such cultural differences has grown among advertising consultancies.

It would appear then that little has changed in this regard in the last seven years. Recently, a professional dialogue between some of the main global advertising companies concluded that recruitment markets still operate differently with regard to the use of the web, and there are wide variations in the costs of getting online across countries and levels of access from home. There are also different cultural attitudes, such as those outlined above, that still influence behaviour in recruitment markets. The advertising industry feels that there is a paradox here, in that organisations have to introduce elements of localisation into the strategy if globalised recruitment policies are to stand any chance of success.[1] Many organisations deal with this by applying 'a light touch' from the centre, having a lead agency responsible for global themes to their recruitment process (such as the pursuit of global employer brands), but also appointing a series of local agencies that can influence how campaigns are run in specific geographies.

CROSS-CULTURAL PSYCHOLOGICAL TESTING

Psychological assessment increasingly involves the application of tests in different cultural contexts, either in a single country (involving migrants) or in different countries ... In the near future the demand for cross-cultural assessment will increase, due to the growing internationalisation of business and the increasing need of migrant groups for culture-informed psychological services.[2]

Developing culture-free, culture-fair and more recently culture-reduced instruments has long been a goal for psychologists.

Where it is accepted that existing instruments are invalid, unreliable or do not cover the construct they are intended for when used in a different cultural setting, then developing culture-specific variations becomes an alternative. This can be costly, so is it necessary and is it cost-effective? Does adaptation add sufficient incremental value to the bad, but common, practice of straightforward applications of existing tests and their norms? The answer to the first part of this question involves more than immediate concerns about fairness and discrimination.

> '...being sure that linguistic capability is being assessed at an appropriate level is never easy.'

It is interesting to note that the issue of assessing English language capability is important both to the South East London NHS Trust and the BBC World Service. In both cases – and for organisations in other sectors – the issue is one of relative risk of miscommunication. Official assessment of linguistic capability is often associated with other processes to help minimise such risks. Indeed, experience of changes in immigration policy in some countries shows that being sure that linguistic capability is being assessed at an appropriate level is never easy.

For example, the chance of obtaining permanent residency in Australia is increased if a university course has been completed, and there has been a huge growth in foreign student numbers, rising from 9,400 to 17,000 between 2001 and 2004. In 2005, Australia's Immigration Department began requiring students from South Asian countries to sit the International English Language Testing System (IELTS) test, for which a minimum score of 6.0 (on a 10-point scale) gives 20 points towards the 120 needed to qualify for a residency visa. Of 2,655 Chinese who sat the test having already finished their studies (successfully), 45 per cent failed to make the grade. In contrast, only 6 per cent of Indian students failed to meet the standard.[3]

> '...very little work has been done on equating different language versions of psychological tests...'

The test houses report that very little work has been done on equating different language versions of psychological tests, except that by the International Test Commission (ITC). It has developed a series of guidelines to advise on the adaptation of psychological and educational tests for use in various different linguistic and cultural contexts (see list of web resources). The guidelines were developed by a 13-person committee representing a number of international organisations and first presented formally to the ITC in 1999 and published in 2001. Updated guidelines are forthcoming and will be discussed at the July 2006 Conference of the ITC, building upon the latest thinking of researchers, educators, psychologists and policy experts. The ITC believes this issue has become more important as tests are used in more and more countries, and tests developed in one country get translated or adapted for use in another.

Some high-visibility cross-national studies, such as the OECD/PISA study of educational attainment of 15-year-olds, requires that there is proper interpretation of tests. Adaptation needs to consider the whole cultural context within which a test is to be used, and consequently the guidelines are relevant even when no translation is involved. Twenty-two guidelines emerged from the project,[4] falling into four categories: the cultural context; technicalities of instrument development and adaptation; test administration; and documentation and interpretation. Excepting the technicalities of instrument development, these all have implications for test use by organisations and test users.

WHERE CAN I FIND OUT MORE?

The International Test Commission (ITC) has a series of guidelines to advise on the adaptation of psychological and educational tests for use in various different linguistic and cultural contexts:

http://www.intestcom.org/ itc_projects.htm#ITC%20Guidelines%20on%20Adapting%20Tests

---

INTERNATIONAL DIFFERENCES IN THE USE OF SELECTION TECHNIQUES

It is clear that HRBPs need to be aware not just of issues of cross-cultural sensitivity of advertising and cross-cultural fairness of testing. There have been a number of studies that have looked at international differences in selection practices and the role of national culture in explaining such differences in desirability and usage. One study examined data from 13 countries using the Best International Human Resource Management Practices Survey to establish whether significant differences existed between nations in terms of commonly used hiring practices. A second study surveying 959 organisations from 20 countries has been used to assess whether differences in staffing practices are due to international differences in some of the factors mentioned above (for example legislation, labour market factors) or to national cultural values.[5] More than half of the organisations operated in multiple countries. It looked at the extent to which 11 core practices (the number of selection methods used, extent of usage, number of verification methods, extent of verification, number of interviews, number of test types, extent of testing, audit process, use of fixed questions, use of peers as interviewers, and use of peers as decision-makers) were used across the countries and in relation to the cultural values of that country.

It was shown that two cultural values (uncertainty avoidance and power distance) could predict some of the practices. Cultures high in uncertainty avoidance used more test types, used them more extensively, conducted more interviews and audited their processes to a greater extent. For example, 11% of variation in the number of verification methods could be linked to scores on uncertainty avoidance and 5% to scores on power distance. Differences were also found in the use of fixed sets of interview questions or structured interviews, either due to a 'technology lag', whereby information on the effectiveness of certain tools and techniques slowly filters across countries, or (more probably) due to the fact that certain cultures find that the idea of structured interviews does not sit well with how to conduct interpersonal interactions and the extent to which one should trust the judgement of the interviewer.

The study concluded:

> National differences accounted for considerable variance in selection practices. This suggests that those attempting to implement standardised worldwide selection practices may face difficulties beyond the known problems of establishing translation equivalence of test and interview materials ... The identification of staffing practices that 'travel well' is needed ... Practices with universal appeal may be easier starting points for those pursuing global selection strategies, but these may not be the 'best practice'. We need to enhance our understanding of the many practical issues associated with global selection systems.[6]

ENDNOTES

1 Glover, C. (2002) Global voice, local accent. *People Management*. 27 June. 40.

2 Van de Vijver, F.J.R. (2002) Cross-cultural assessment: value for money? *Applied Psychologist: An International Review*. Vol. 51, No. 4. 545–66, p.545.

3 Masten, G. (2006) Chinese puzzle over Australian visa test failure rate. *Time Higher Education*. 20 January.12. Research conducted by Dr Bob Birrell, Monash University for the Immigration Department. He is a member of NPC Working Party on Immigration Selection in 1988, which led to the reform of the migration selection system introduced in 1989. He is a member of the panel of experts which is reviewing the General Skilled Migration Categories for the Commonwealth Government, appointed in mid-2005.

4 See: Hambleton, R.K. (1994) Guidelines for adapting educational and psychological tests: a progress report. *European Journal of Psychological Assessment* (Bulletin of the International Test Commission). Vol. 10. 229–44. Van de Vijver, F.J.R. and Hambleton, R.K. (1996) Translating tests: some practical guidelines. *European Psychologist*. Vol. 1. 89–99.

5 See for example: Ryan, A.M., McFarland, L., Baron, H. and Page, R. (1999) An international look at selection practices: nation and culture as explanations for variability in practice. *Personnel Psychology*. Vol. 52. 359–91; Huo, Y.P., Huang, H.J. and Napier, N.K. (2002) Divergence or convergence: a cross-national comparison of personnel selection practices. *Human Resource Management*. Vol. 41, No. 1. 31–44.

6 Ryan, A.M., McFarland, L., Baron, H. and Page, R. (1999) An international look at selection practices: nation and culture as explanations for variability in practice. *Personnel Psychology*. Vol. 52. 359–91, p. 385.

CONCLUSION

14

Seven years ago if you asked the question, 'who is your expert on international recruitment, selection and assessment?' you probably would have been directed to someone inside a specialised function dealing with internationally mobile employees such as expatriates. However, in the context of skills shortages, immigration, global talent management and rapid international expansion, this expertise has become much more spread out inside the organisation and it is applied to a much wider range of employees. Organisations are having to globalise most of their basic HR processes – and this includes those concerned with recruitment, selection and assessment – and this globalisation is creating new roles and new activity streams inside the HR function. In addition to being able to manage international employees such as expatriates, HR functions now also have to be able to passively attract self-initiated movers in an international labour market, to actively capitalise on immigration and the skills they bring, to transfer knowledge from centres of excellence and to make those centres build globally relevant skills, or to outsource specific recruitment, selection and assessment activities.

The HR function has to be able to co-ordinate the activity that takes place across what are in practice multiple methods of resourcing international business. Although many of the technical debates around the standard tools and techniques involved – candidate engagement, advertising, use of headhunters, graduate programmes, candidate screening, testing, assessment and socialisation of international employees - are little changed over the years, the context within which international recruitment, selection and assessment takes place has changed profoundly. The new context includes: the transfer of work abroad (either to outsourced providers or on a global in-sourcing basis); the e-enablement of many HR processes; greater sophistication in HR information technology; changes in the structure of International HR functions; more competition for talented staff at all levels of organisation; more protracted and strategic talent pipeline; and the challenge of attracting international labour to home markets from new and often little understood labour pools.

It is clear that recruitment, selection and assessment philosophies generalise internationally, but the detail of the processes involved generally does not. There is a continuing need for organisations to understand the local and cultural context that surrounds. A number of issues place considerable boundaries around what an organisation can do in its activity in this area:

❖ Global labour supply patterns (geography), immigration rules etc

❖ The legislative context surrounding local labour markets

❖ The qualifications, language skills, implicit capabilities, retention/career advancement behaviour of candidates

❖ The use of specific recruitment, selection and assessment tools and techniques

❖ Competencies at the level of behavioural indicators and what can be assessed by psychological tests

❖ Employee engagement behaviour and drivers across countries, employee 'buy-in' to specific values, and the labour market behaviour around various employee value propositions.

However, in addition to understanding these local sensitivities, organisations must also create themes that bring a sense of relevance and co-ordination to their recruitment, selection and assessment activities across the various countries in which they operate. The research identified three such themes:

❖ The use of core strategic competencies that differentiate the firm, which are then pushed into career development/ performance management systems

❖ The pursuit of talent management/skills supply initiatives on a more global basis, which in turn necessitates: the need to research consumer insights; develop business models that enable the HR function to recruit 'ahead of the curve'; ensure consistency in communication and employment brand messages; develop distributed centres of excellence for recruitment, selection and assessment services as well as centres of excellence that can take control of the skill formation process for key employee groups; improve the efficiency, effectiveness and strategic control over global supplier provision; develop pools of international assessors; and e-enable much of the transactional recruitment, selection and assessment activity

❖ The building of corporate and global brands (the image and reputation of the organisation) and the exploration of the ways in which employees from very different cultural and national backgrounds can still identify with and support the brand.

Another conclusion that can be drawn from the research is that in some of these areas, there is a temptation for the rhetoric and the desire to develop more effective global co-ordination to outstrip

the ability of HR professionals to actually deliver such a strategy in each of the countries involved. An example covered in the report is that of employment branding. In practice a range of factors to do with the organisation's international expansion strategy and local labour market behaviour can make it extremely difficult to develop generalisable themes across different country operations.

Organisations are however learning how to co-ordinate such activities quickly. The added value of HR function when handling international recruitment, selection and assessment lies in its ability to manage the delicate balance between globally co-ordinated systems and sensitivity to local needs in a way that aligns with business needs and senior management philosophy. The research shows that there is clearly now a distinction to be made between international HRM and global HRM. Where organisations have gone through this learning, it becomes clear that they manage the recruitment, selection and assessment activities hand in hand with changes in management development and reward. The old divides between these international functions have become increasingly weak.